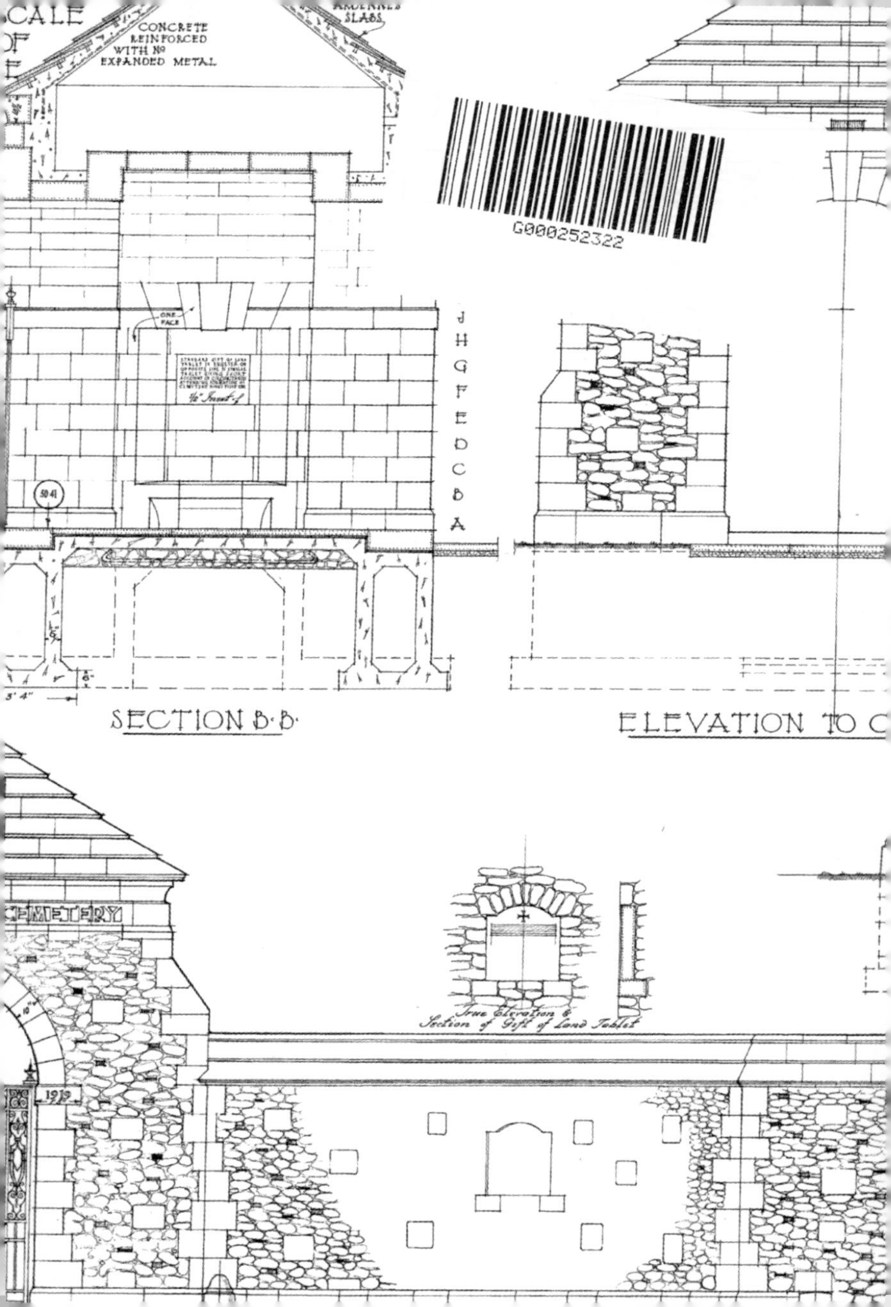
SCALE
CONCRETE
REINFORCED
WITH No
EXPANDED METAL
SLABS
ONE FACE
G000252322
J
H
G
F
E
D
C
B
A
SECTION B-B
ELEVATION TO C
True Elevation &
Section of Gift of Land Tablet
CEMETERY
1919

Epitaphs of the Great War: Passchendaele

This book is dedicated to my
children, their grandfathers
who fought in Burma,
North Africa and Italy, and to
my grandchildren.

EPITAPHS OF THE GREAT WAR: PASSCHENDAELE

SARAH WEARNE

1917
2017

Uniform
an imprint of Unicorn Publishing Group

Unicorn Publishing Group
101 Wardour Street
London W1F 0UG
www.unicornpublishing.org

First published by Uniform 2017

A CIP catalogue record for this book is available from the British Library

ISBN 978-1-910500-65-1

Printed and bound in Czech Republic

Photograph on pages 10-11: Commonwealth War Graves Commission
Photographs on pages 18-9, 23, 27, 36-7, 39, 47, 51, 67, 95, 117, 119, 126-7: James Kerr
Photograph page 91: Sarah Wearne

Acknowledgements

I should like to thank Glyn Prysor and Max Dutton at the Commonwealth War Graves Commission for their help with my research; James Kerr for permission to use his photographs of the Passchendaele cemeteries, and Ryan Gearing of Unicorn Publishing Group whose idea it was to turn my blog www.epitaphsofthegreatwar.com into books. The books would not have happened had my son, Harry Wearne, not built and supported the website and its associated Twitter account @WWInscriptions for which I am very grateful. As I am to my husband whose support, company and encouragement over many years has been invaluable.

THE BATTLE OF PASSCHENDAELE (THIRD YPRES)

CAMPAIGNS 31 JULY – 10 NOVEMBER 1917

31 July 1917 - Battle of Pilckem Ridge

10 August 1917 - Capture of Westhoek

16 August 1917 - Battle of Langemarck

20-25 September 1917 - Battle of the Menin Road

26 September – 3 October 1917 - Battle of Polygon Wood

4 October 1917 - Battle of Broodseinde

9 October 1917 - Battle of Poelcappelle

12 October 1917 - First Battle of Passchendaele

26 October – 10 November 1917 - Second Battle of Passchendaele

PREFACE

Allowed sixty-six characters to compose a personal inscription for the grave of your son or husband what on earth would you say? Especially if this was going to be the only contribution you could make to his burial and commemoration, you had not been with him when he died, not seen him when he was dead and were unlikely ever to be able to visit his grave. The pressure to say something significant must have been enormous. Many people fell back on conventional phrases – Rest in peace, Thy will be done, Not lost but gone before – but some found beautiful, original and profound ways to express themselves. Not that today we fully understand what they were saying. Forced by the letter count to be brief, many inscriptions are consequently cryptic, making it difficult for us to understand what they were saying since we don't recognise the quotes or pick up the allusions in the way that contemporaries would have done.

This book looks at one hundred inscriptions, chosen from the graves of one nursing sister and ninety-nine British, Australian, Canadian and South African soldiers who all died in the service of King George V during the Battle of Passchendaele, 31 July to 10 November 1917. Drawing out their threads, placing the inscriptions in their context, takes us into the hearts, minds and lives of the wartime generation, of those who lived through the war, died in the war, and of those who mourned its dead.

Flanders was an unforgiving battlefield; if ever soldiers struggled in the slime it was here. And they didn't just struggle in it they drowned in it. Pulverised by shells and swallowed by the mud, many men's bodies disappeared without trace, their names among the 34,887 missing dead carved onto the walls of Tyne Cot Memorial, or the 54,395 on the Menin Gate.

Realising the importance families would place on knowing where their dead were buried, the Graves Registration Unit searched out and marked graves with their wooden crosses, recording the map references so they would be able to locate them again when the war was over. And after the war it scoured the battlefields, locating bodies, identifying them where they could and then burying them in what were to become the permanent cemeteries. Once they had done this, the bodies became the responsibility of the Imperial War Graves Commission, which had been founded in 1917 to construct and maintain the cemeteries 'in perpetuity'.

Unidentified bodies predominate in the frontline cemeteries. At Tyne Cot 70% of the 11,961 burials are unidentified, at Passchendaele New British Cemetery it's 76%. Row upon row of graves bear the same inscription: 'An Unknown Soldier of the Great War

– Known unto God'. Wounded soldiers were passed down a casualty evacuation chain that began at the regimental aid posts, just behind the front line, and ended, for the most seriously wounded, in Britain. Cemeteries accompany each stage of this journey; the further the cemetery from the front line the greater the number of identified burials. But it's a tribute to the efficiency of the system that some men who died in Casualty Clearing Stations, which could be 20 km behind the front line, had only been wounded a few hours earlier.

The repatriation of bodies had been forbidden during the war, and remained in force once the war was over – even if relations offered to pay, which many did. The War Graves Commission argued that to allow those who could afford it to bring the bodies of their dead home would separate the rich from the poor, leaving the war cemeteries as the equivalent of paupers' graveyards. It was determined its cemeteries should be the symbol of a great imperial army that had fought and died together. To this end the Commission made another decision: to ban private headstones. Even if you had already put one up you were going to have to take it down. The headstones were to be of a uniform size and shape – a curve-topped rectangular stone – to emphasise the equality of sacrifice of all soldiers regardless of their military rank or station in life. Both decisions were extremely controversial leading a great many people to demand to know what freedom they had all been fighting for if they were now going to have to submit to the tyranny of the state in this way.

Each headstone was to be carved with the casualty's name, age, regiment, regimental number, regimental badge and date of death. However, it took years to construct the cemeteries and it could be 1924 or even later before relatives were asked to check the details on the Family Verification Form, suggest an inscription and say whether they wanted a religious emblem on the headstone, a cross or a Star of David. This is one of the reasons why so many graves do not have an inscription; families had moved on without leaving forwarding addresses. This and the fact that the Commission charged relatives 3½d a letter, making them too expensive for some next-of-kin. The New Zealand Government, feeling that this infringed the Commission's principle of equality, refused to allow any inscriptions on their graves. The Canadian Government, for exactly the same reason, decided it would pay for all theirs. Nevertheless, there are many Canadian headstones without an inscription because, as in Britain, so much time had passed that families could no longer be contacted.

For all that the War Graves Commission was intransigent over the repatriation of bodies and the design of the headstone – even when people accepted the principle of uniformity they still fought furiously for it to be a cross – it seems to have been remarkably lenient when it came to enforcing some of its other rules. There is evidence of families being excused the charge; there are plenty of inscriptions that exceed the sixty-six character limit, some having well over a hundred. And despite the fact that the rules say no foreign alphabets can be accepted there is more than one Hebrew inscription, and even one consisting of musical notation. The Commission was perhaps more concerned to ensure that no inscriptions insulted the Germans – or the British for that matter. But it did allow plenty that were critical of war: 'Man's inhumanity to man makes countless thousands mourn', 'Sacrificed to the fallacy that war can end war'. It was happy to exercise discretion in order to achieve its harmonious vision.

Just over 20% of graves have inscriptions: 211,655 out of almost 1 million dead. An analysis of what they say reveals that a great many people believed they would meet their loved ones again when they too died; that a vast number were prepared to accept their fate as being the will of God; that duty was the greatest motivator; Tennyson the most popular poet; that the British Army was a polyglot army, its soldiers speaking languages as diverse as Welsh, Finnish and Afrikaans, and that whilst relations lauded heroism and spoke of glory the soldiers themselves admired cheerfulness and coolness under fire. Soldiers died for 'King and Country', for Australia, Scotland or 'the honour of Bristol', for freedom, civilization or liberty, some 'to end war', one for the 'greatest cause in history', one for 'his wife and little son'. There is no single narrative.

Sarah Wearne
May 2017

The inscriptions in this book have been chosen from my blog – www.epitaphsofthegreatwar.com. This links to the Twitter site – @WWInscriptions – to which a new inscription is posted at 5.30 every evening of the First World War Centenary, 4 August 2014 to 11 November 2018.

Tyne Cot Cemetery with the original Graves Registration Unit wooden crosses. Photo courtesy of CWGC

The odds and ends He loved so well All left behind

PRIVATE GEORGE RIDLEY LESLIE
LEINSTER REGIMENT
DIED 31 JULY 1917 AGED 20
BURIED POTIJZE CHATEAU LAWN CEMETERY, BELGIUM

Private Leslie was killed on the opening day of the Third Ypres campaign. Although his battalion, the 7th Leinsters, were in reserve, Leslie was among a party of about 500 men detailed to dig a trench and bury a cable that would connect up the forward communications as the battle progressed. At 9.15 am they reached Potijze Chateau where the enemy guns covered the ground. The regimental history records that whilst they were 'proceeding up the Potijze road the party came under heavy shrapnel fire, and a number of casualties occurred'. This included one officer and 33 soldiers wounded and ten soldiers killed. Private Leslie was among those killed.

His mother, Mrs Annie Leslie, composed a wonderfully original inscription for her son's headstone, all the more poignant for its vivid informality. Leslie, who was born in Glasgow, had been a golf groundsman in Wellingborough before the war.

And how can man die better Than facing fearful odds

LIEUTENANT CARL HANSEN
MACHINE GUN CORPS ATTD THE KING'S (LIVERPOOL REGIMENT)
DIED 31 JULY 1917 AGED 24
BURIED IN POTIJZE CHATEAU LAWN CEMETERY

Lord Macaulay asks this question in the first lines of *Horatius at the Bridge*, a stalwart of nineteenth-century poetry anthologies. Horatius risks his life to save Rome, reasoning:

> To every men upon this earth
> Death cometh soon or late.
> And how can man die better
> Than facing fearful odds
> For the ashes of his fathers
> And the temples of his gods.

The odds were certainly against Hansen and his Lewis gun team on the 31 July. There is no individual information about his fate but the battalion war diary recorded that:

> Four minutes after zero, the enemy put a heavy barrage of H.E. shells on Oxford Trench – several men were hit there, a Lewis Gun team was knocked out, and the reserve Lewis Gun ammunition blown up.

The war diary is as always briefly factual but *The Valley of the Shadow – 31 July 1917*, a poem by the battalion's commanding officer, Major E.G. Hoare, leaves little to the imagination. This is the third verse:

> Down in the valley the barrage fell,
> Fountains of water and steel and smoke,
> Screams of demons and blast of hell,
> The flash that binds and the fumes that choke.
> The mud and the wire have chained the feet,
> You are up to your knees in swamp and slime,
> There's a laugh when the crossing is once complete,
> But a setting of teeth for the second time.

Y PRIFARDD HEDD WYNN

PRIVATE ELLIS HUMPHREY EVANS
ROYAL WELSH FUSILIERS
DIED 31 JULY 1917 AGED 30
BURIED ARTILLERY WOOD CEMETERY

Ellis Humphrey Evans was reluctant to be a soldier. Not only was he a Welsh non-conformist who remained true to its firm pacifist beliefs, but he was a shepherd on his father's farm and therefore involved in work of national importance – producing food for the nation. However, with the introduction of conscription in January 1916 either he or his brother had to join up and Ellis decided that as the elder brother it should be him.

In June 1917 he joined the 15th Battalion the Royal Welsh Fusiliers in France and at the end of July was killed in the Battle of Pilkhem Ridge. His inscription – Y prifardd Hedd Wyn – reveals him to be the Chief Bard Hedd Wyn whose poem, *Yr Arwr* (The Hero), written whilst he was in the army, led to him being posthumously awarded the bardic chair at the National Eisteddfod.

In 1923 his home town of Trawsfynydd in Merionydd erected a statue to his memory showing the poet as a shepherd not as a soldier. Below the statue is a bronze plaque inscribed with the details of his death and below that an 'englyn', a short piece of verse, which Evans wrote in memory of a friend killed in action in 1916:

Ei aberth nid a heibio- ei wyneb
Annwyl nid a'n ango
Er i'r Almaen ystaenio
Ei dwrn dur yn ei waed o

This translates as: 'His sacrifice and his dear face will not be forgotten even though Germany has stained her fist of steel in his blood'.

4TH SON OF EARL OF ALBEMARLE KILLED IN ACTION WESTHOEK MENTIONED IN DESPATCHES RESURGAM

LIEUTENANT THE HON. ALBERT EDWARD KEPPEL
RIFLE BRIGADE
DIED 31 JULY 1917 AGED 19
BURIED IN AEROPLANE CEMETERY

The Times Thursday 23 August 1917

A correspondent signing himself "X" writes of Lieutenant Albert Edward George Arnold Keppel, Rifle Brigade, whose death was briefly recorded in *The Times* of August 7: Lieutenant Keppel was killed in action on 31 July while gallantly leading his men in a counter-attack, before which the Germans were retiring. He was the youngest of Lord and Lady Albemarle's four sons serving in the present war. It is safe to say that many a tear will be shed in his memory; many a pulse will quicken when it is known how and where this gay and débonaire spirit vanished from our midst. Both at Ludgrove and later at Eton, that he loved so well, he gave promise of future success in the playing fields, but left Eton early, at his own wish, in order to join the Army. He was never very much captivated by the study of his books, but had an extraordinary aptitude for picking up a fund of general information. During his short life, from his earliest childhood, his high spirits and joie de vivre gave an impression of sunshine and joy wherever he went, and this is shown in the dark hour of his death by the spontaneous testimony of many of his companions, both boys and girls, not to mention older people, officers of standing in the Army, and the pastors and masters under whose guidance he so lightly trod the paths of this world here below.'

His commanding officer writes: 'He was perfectly splendid in the attack, and was killed by a rifle bullet whilst running forward with a Lewis gun which he was about to use on some Germans who were running away ... His body is, I am afraid, up to the present not yet buried, as, after a swaying fight, the ground where he fell changed hands'.

A brother-officer writes: - 'He was last seen chasing a German through some undergrowth, where he was killed either by machine-gun or a sniper. I do not think anything speaks more for his gallantry than the fact that the ground where he fell was never really held by us; he was so far ahead at the time.'

"MY SON, MY SON" "NO REWARD CAN BE TOO GREAT"

CAPTAIN THOMAS RIVERSDALE COLYER-FERGUSSON VC
NORTHAMPTONSHIRE REGIMENT
DIED 31 JULY 1917 AGED 21
BURIED IN MENIN ROAD SOUTH MILITARY CEMETERY

Captain Colyer-Fergusson's father quoted from two separate sources for his son's inscription. The first line comes from the Old Testament, 2 Samuel 18:33. These are the words King David speaks when he hears of the death of his rebel son, Absalom:

> And the King was much moved, and went up to the chamber over the gate, and wept: and as he went, thus he said, O my son Absalom, my son, my son Absalom! would God I had died for thee, O Absalom, my son, my son!

The second quotation comes from the citation for his son's Victoria Cross, awarded for his actions on the day he was killed:

> For most conspicuous bravery, skilful leading and determination in attack. The tactical situation having developed contrary to expectation, it was not possible for his company to adhere to the original plan of deployments, and owing to the difficulties of the ground and to enemy wire, Captain Colyer Fergusson found himself with a Sergeant and five men only. He carried out the attack nevertheless, and succeeded in capturing the enemy trench and disposing of the garrison. His party was then threatened by a heavy counter-attack from the left front, but this attack he successfully resisted. During this operation, assisted by his Orderly only, he attacked and captured an enemy machine gun and turned it on the assailants, many of whom were killed and a large number driven into the hands of an adjoining British unit. Later, assisted only by his Serjeant, he again attacked and captured a second enemy machine gun, by which time he had been joined by other portions of his company, and was enabled to consolidate his position. The conduct of this officer throughout forms an amazing record of dash, gallantry and skill, for which no reward can be too great, having regard to the importance of the position won. This gallant officer was shortly afterwards killed by a sniper.

PASS FRIEND – ALL'S WELL!

LIEUTENANT STEPHEN REGINALD PARKE WALTER
ROYAL FLYING CORPS
DIED 31 JULY 1917 AGED 20
BURIED LIJSSENTHOEK MILITARY CEMETERY

'Pass friend – all's well!' is the sentry's response to someone who gives the correct reply to his challenge: 'Halt, who goes there!' As an inscription it has a double sense: that we who pass by are able to do so because those who died made it safe for us, and that those who died correctly met the challenge of life and have therefore been allowed to pass into eternal life.

The line appears as a refrain in a Harrow School song, of which this is the second verse:

> You stand where your brothers stood,
> And pray where your brothers prayed,
> Who fought with Death as brave men should,
> Not boasting and not afraid.
> For the blood and the lives that your brothers gave,
> For the glory that you share,
> The message comes from beyond the grave,
> The challenge "Who goes there - you?
> Pass, Friend, All's well."

Twenty-year-old Stephen Walter, an ace, flew with 32 Squadron and achieved six victories between the 11th and the 28th July 1917. He was killed near Vlamertinghe on the morning of the 31st. His plane took off at 6.05 am with four others to take part in an offensive patrol. It was pouring with rain and the cloud base was only 1,000 ft. In the poor visibility an unseen kite balloon cable sheered of his port wings causing the plane to break up and crash. He was his parents' only child.

Lijssenthoek
Military
Cemetery

He gave up all
Even life itself
For the ideals
Of truth and justice

SECOND LIEUTENANT ARNOLD WILLIAM RASH
SUFFOLK REGIMENT
DIED 31 JULY 1917 AGED 25
BURIED IN BUFFS ROAD CEMETERY

To the Greek philosopher, Socrates (469-399 BC), truth and justice were not only inseparable but both were essential for good government. Socrates didn't mean justice as an external force applied for the maintenance of law and order but as a quality attained by those who truthfully examined and understood themselves, considering that it was this that made them fit for leadership. Almost two and a half thousand years later, truth and justice are still considered to be ideals for a good society. Socrates refused to compromise his principles, even though the alternative was certain death. Mrs Mary Rash, Second Lieutenant Rash's mother who chose his inscription, implies the same attachment to principle in her son's determination to fight. Arnold Rash was already a territorial soldier when the war broke out. He belonged to the 4th Battalion the Suffolk Regiment and went with it to France in November 1914, serving with them continuously until he returned to take a commission in October 1915. The War Graves Commission has him serving with the 5th Battalion the Suffolk Regiment, but he was with the Cambridgeshire Regiment when he was killed. Arnold's younger brother, Ralph, was killed on the Somme on 12 October 1916 aged 19. His body was never recovered and he is commemorated on the Thiepval Memorial.

BUT THE THOUSANDTH MAN WILL STAND YOUR FRIEND WITH THE WHOLE ROUND WORLD AGIN YOU

SECOND LIEUTENANT HERBERT C ROSA
ROYAL FIELD ARTILLERY
DIED 31 JULY 1917 AGED 33
BURIED POPERINGHE NEW MILITARY CEMETERY

Herbert Rosa's wife chose his inscription. It comes from Rudyard Kipling's poem, *The Thousandth Man*. The thousandth man is an exceptional person, more close than a brother he believes in you, sees you for what you are, always stands by you and is utterly trustworthy.

> Nine hundred and ninety-nine depend
> On what the world sees in you,
> But the Thousandth Man will stand your friend
> With the whole round world agin you.

Rosa was born in Hammersmith, London three years before his father, Carl Rosa, 'a natural born subject of the Empire of Germany', became a naturalised British citizen. Educated at Clifton College, on leaving school he became a tea merchant in London and a member of the Honourable Artillery Company. When the war broke out Rosa was living in Ireland but re-joined the HAC and served with them in Egypt, returning to take a commission in the Royal Field Artillery in 1916, serving with the 8th Division Ammunition Column. Wounded in action near Wytschaete, he died in a Field Ambulance dressing station in Poperinghe.

> Nine hundred and ninety-nine can't bide
> The shame or mocking laughter,
> But the Thousandth Man will stand by your side
> To the gallows-foot – and after!

Of Bryngwenallt Dolgelly, N. Wales "A ddug angau ni ddwg angof"

SECOND LIEUTENANT GRIFFITH CHRISTMAS OWEN
SOUTH WALES BORDERERS
DIED 31 JULY 1917 AGED 30
BURIED SANCTUARY WOOD CEMETERY

Griffith Christmas Owen's inscription 'A ddug angau ni ddwg angof', when death comes it does not mean we forget, is quoted from the dedication on the war memorial in his home town – Dolgellau (Dolgelly). Griffith was killed on 31 July 1917 leading his men in an assault on Pilckem Ridge. The South Wales Borderers lost 320 men killed, wounded and missing between 31 July and 2 August. Owen was among the missing; his body not discovered until 24 April 1928.

This was nine months after the inauguration of the Menin Gate, which commemorates 54,620 officers and men 'who fell in Ypres Salient, but to whom the fortune of war denied the known and honoured burial given to their comrades in death', of whom Griffith Christmas Owen was thought to be one.

However, not only was Owen's body discovered in 1928 but it proved possible to identify it – from its 'badge of rank and general service clothing'. Consequently Owen now has a grave in Sanctuary Wood Cemetery, and an inscription chosen by his brother John Llewellyn Owen.

Sanctuary Wood Cemetery

HIS COUNTRY CALLED
HE ANSWERED

LANCE CORPORAL DOUGLAS GILRUTH HENDERSON
SCOTS GUARDS
DIED 1 AUGUST 1917 AGED 19
BURIED IN MENDINGHEM MILITARY CEMETERY

The First World War threw up a new style of mourning jewellery, an oval locket with the words 'His country called, he answered' inscribed around the frame holding the photograph of 'your' soldier. Anyone who volunteered was deemed 'to have answered the call', but the term was usually reserved for those who had answered the call with their lives.

What was 'the call'? It was the call to arms, the call to take up arms in defence of your country. Kitchener issued the first 'call' within days of the outbreak of the war; a 'Call to arms' for an additional 100,000 men 'in this present National Emergency'. Later the term was used more loosely on recruiting posters, like the one headed 'Your country's call', which shows a kilted soldier gesturing to a quintessentially English thatched cottage and asking 'Isn't this worth fighting for?'

The phrase frequently featured in *In Memoriam* verse:

> His country called – he answered
> Old England to defend
> Mid shot and shell he never swerved
> Faced duty to the end.
> When death is near and all seems night
> May we like him say, "It's all right".

Other examples are no better.

Douglas Henderson was a volunteer; his medal card shows that he received the 1914-15 Star, qualifying for it on 8 April 1915. As he was only 2 in the 1901 census, this means that he can have been no older than 17 in April 1915. Wounded twice, in 1915 and 1916, he was wounded again on 31 July and died the next day.

[25]

COULD I BUT KNEEL BESIDE THE GRAVE OF HIM WE LOVED SO DEAR HIS MOTHER

BOMBARDIER WILLIAM J SWETMAN
ROYAL FIELD ARTILLERY
DIED 2 AUGUST 1917 AGED 29
BURIED BELGIAN BATTERY CORNER CEMETERY

There were two reasons why Mrs Swetman couldn't kneel beside her son's grave: one, the army had forbidden the repatriation of bodies and two, the cost and complication of visiting his grave in Belgium would have been beyond her means.

The army's decision not to repatriate bodies during the war had been understandable: it was a waste of resources and manpower. In addition, recovering the bodies of the dead encouraged soldiers to take needless risks. Forbidding the repatriation of bodies once the war was over was about equality. It would have been far too expensive for the Government to repatriate the dead, but if it allowed individuals to pay to bring their dead home that would mean the rich dead were being separated from the poor, something the Imperial War Graves Commission was determined shouldn't happen since its aim was that the cemeteries should be the outward symbol of a great army that had fought and died together, and was buried together.

The refusal to repatriate her son's body meant that Mrs Swetman could never kneel beside his grave in England, but a visit to her his grave in Belgium wouldn't necessarily have been beyond her means. Once the war was over organizations sprang up to facilitate such visits. The St Barnabas Society, established in 1919, set up group trips, which reduced the cost so that poorer families might be able to afford them, and after 1921 it organised an annual free trip, you just needed to be a genuine applicant and be prepared to write a few lines afterwards for the Society's records. All the logistics, special passes, passports, travel and accommodation were taken care of. And at the other end of the spectrum, Thomas Cook and Michelin began to organise battlefield tours both for relations and for tourists who started to arrive in increasingly large numbers.

William Swetman was a regular soldier. The 1911 census shows him to have been serving with the 84th Battery RFA in 'Ceylon and India'. It had returned to England by the time war broke out and arrived in France on 6 November 1914, enabling Swetman to qualify for the 1914 Star.

"THE ELEMENTS BE KIND TO THEE AND MAKE THY SPIRITS ALL OF COMFORT"

S

LIEUTENANT ARNOLD GRAYSON BLOOMER
LINCOLNSHIRE REGIMENT
DIED 3 AUGUST 1917 AGED 31
BURIED BRANDHOEK NEW MILITARY CEMETERY

> *Birmingham Daily Post* 9 August 1917
> Lieutenant Arnold Grayson Bloomer of the Lincolns, who received a mortal wound on 31 July, was the second son of Mr. and Mrs. G.F. Bloomer of Stratford-on-Avon, and grandson of the late Mr. George Yates, surgeon of Birmingham. He was educated at King Edward VI's School, Stratford-on-Avon, and on the outbreak of war he joined a Birmingham City Battalion. After training he was given a commission and went to France, where he remained for about 18 months. He came home on sick leave, under-went a serious operation, and returned to France in May last. He was 31 years of age.

Arnold Bloomer's inscription comes from Shakespeare's *Antony and Cleopatra*, an appropriate source for someone who was educated at Shakespeare's own school. They are the words Octavius speaks to his sister Octavia as she leaves Rome with her new husband, Antony:

> Farewell, my dearest sister, fare thee well:
> The elements be kind to thee, and make
> Thy spirits all of comfort, fare thee well.

Bloomer was mortally wounded on the opening day of the Passchendaele Campaign. He died three days later in a Casualty Clearing Station in Brandhoek after, his parents were assured, receiving 'all possible care and attention'.

BRANDHOEK
NEW MILITARY
CEMETERY

Omnia vincit amor

CAPTAIN CHARLES CADWALADR TREVOR-ROPER
HAMPSHIRE REGIMENT
DIED 3 AUGUST 1917 AGED 33
BURIED DUHALLOW A.D.S. CEMETERY

Charles Trevor-Roper was an actor. After taking his degree at Clare College, Cambridge he went on to study at the Academy of Dramatic Art. During the winter of 1911 he toured Australia with Harry Irving's company, and at the outbreak of war was playing Captain Felix in *The Grande Seigneur* at the Savoy Theatre.

In 1901, following the death of an uncle, Trevor-Roper inherited the family estate of Plas Teg in Flintshire, together with a large fortune. Although he was the eleventh of twelve children, his elder siblings were all girls. The twelfth child was also a boy, Geoffrey; he too was killed in the war.

Trevor-Roper's wife chose his inscription – Omnia vincit amor. It comes from Virgil's *Eclogue X*, line 69 – Love conquers all things. The Trevor-Roper's only son, Richard, who had been the rear gunner in Guy Gibson's Lancaster bomber during the Dambusters Raid, 16/17 May 1943, was killed in action in another raid over Germany on 31 March 1944.

"Servant of God, man's friend"

MAJOR ARTHUR TOWARD WATSON
KING'S ROYAL RIFLE CORPS
DIED 5 AUGUST 1917 AGED 47
BURIED LA CLYTTE MILITARY CEMETERY

There is a black marble plaque in St Andrew's Church, Bishopthorpe, Selby, Yorkshire, which tells the story of Major Watson's war:

> To the beloved memory of Arthur Toward Watson Major 21st Battn. Kings Royal Rifles of Bishopthorpe Garth and of Burnopfield in the County of Durham. He offered his services to his Country as a soldier in the Great War. He led a company in the Battle of the Somme, Sept. 15th 1916, when he was severely wounded, and in the Battle of Messines on June 7th 1917. On Sunday Aug. 5th 1917, when second in command of his Battn. he was killed in action in the fighting for Passchendaele Ridge in his 48th year

Arthur Watson was a wealthy coal owner. He had always wanted a career in the army but he was blind in one eye as the result of a non-military gun-shot injury. This had previously prevented him joining the army but it didn't stop him receiving a temporary commission in September 1914. Severely wounded on the Somme, he returned to the front in April 1917. At the beginning of August he received a home posting. He went up the line for one last time to say good-bye to his old battalion and was badly wounded when a shell exploded beside him. He died the next day.

The quotation marks round Watson's inscription are a puzzle. The words don't appear to be a quote, nor does the syntax sound like normal speech. Nevertheless, an inscription on the reredos, also in St Andrew's Church, supports the idea that Watson, in serving God, was a friend to man:

> To the Glory of God & in loving memory of Arthur Toward Watson whose days on earth were spent in the endeavour to make the lives of others happy & who for his King and Country willingly laid down his life in battle. This reredos and panelling were placed in this chancel by Virginia his widow, John his son & Diana his daughter. MCMXIX

ALL THAT HE HAS LEFT
IS BRUISED
AND IRREMEDIABLY BEREFT

LIEUTENANT FREDERIC DOBELL YOUNG
ROYAL GARRISON ARTILLERY
DIED 6 AUGUST 1917 AGED 30
BURIED CANADA FARM CEMETERY

Other relations quoted from this poem, *In Memoriam A.H.* by Maurice Baring, preferring the consolation of, 'That it is well with you ... among the very brave, the very true', to the bleak lines Frederic Young's father chose. Baring wrote the poem in memory of his great friend Auberon Herbert. Like Young's father, he could not believe he would never see or speak to him again.

... The desolated space
Of life shall nevermore
Be what it was before.
No one shall take your place.
No other face
Can fill that empty frame.
There is no answer when we call your name.
We cannot hear your step upon the stair.
We turn to speak and find a vacant chair.
Something is broken which we cannot mend.
God has done more than take away a friend
In taking you; for all that we have left
Is irremediably bereft.
There is none like you.

Young who came from Jesmond, Newcastle-upon-Tyne, originally served as a member of the Tynemouth Battery, a territorial battery, used to guard the coast in the early days of the war. However, once it became obvious that an invasion of Britain was unlikely, these trained batteries were sent overseas. It was 26 July 1917 before Young reached the war zone. He was killed eleven days later.

THE PATH OF DUTY WAS THE WAY TO GLORY

GUNNER LOUIS GOLDIE VICTOR BALDING
ROYAL GARRISON ARTILLERY
DIED 7 AUGUST 1917 AGED 30
BURIED BARD COTTAGE CEMETERY

Tennyson's *Ode on the Death of the Duke of Wellington* offers the assurance that glory is achieved by doing your duty:

> Yea, let all good things await
> Him who cares not to be great,
> But as he saves or serves the state.
> Not once or twice in our rough island story,
> The path of duty was the way to glory.

In 1918, the artist Christopher Nevinson's painting, 'Paths to Glory' showing two dead soldiers face down in the mud was censored by the official censor as being bad for morale. Yet Thomas Gray (1716-1771) would have agreed with Nevinson.

> The boast of heraldry, the pomp of pow'r,
> And all that beauty, all that wealth e'er gave,
> Await alike th' inevitable hour.
> The paths of glory lead but to the grave.
>
> *Elegy Written in a Country Churchyard*

Louis Balding did his duty. Conscription, introduced in March 1916, originally only applied to single men. Balding had got married on 26 December 1915. But in May 1916 it was extended to include married men. Balding joined up in July. He went to the Western Front in October, serving with the 185th Siege Battery RGA and was killed in action, along with three other men from the Battery on 7 August. The path of duty was the way to 'glory' and the path of glory led but to the grave.

HEAVEN IS FULL OF GAY AND CARELESS FACES NEW-WAKED FROM DREAMS OF DREADFUL THINGS

PRIVATE JAMES AULINNE GRAY
ROYAL ARMY MEDICAL CORPS
DIED 9 AUGUST 1917 AGED 17
BURIED BRANDHOEK NEW MILITARY CEMETERY

James Gray joined the army when he was 14; his parents said so in the War Graves Commission's cemetery register. He had been in France since October 1915 by which time he might have been 15. Nevertheless, whether 14 or 15 he was still significantly under age. But, if you looked 18 or 19 the army took your word for it. It was only with the introduction of the National Registration Act in July 1915 that you had to be able to prove your age. Gray served with the 108th Field Ambulance. Two years after his death, the 108th presented a plaque in his memory to the Ormeau Road Methodist Church, Belfast. In his eulogy, Major SB Boyd Campbell told the congregation that James had been a special favourite with them all:

> He could be depended upon at all tims to carry through any work set before him. It was his own desire to take up the dangerous work of stretcher bearer. He faced every risk and nobly died in discharging his duty.

Gray's inscription comes from the second verse of *Flower of Youth*, an immensely popular poem by the Irish poet, Katharine Tynan, first published in *The Spectator* on 26 December 1914. Tynan herself believed that she had written better poetry about the war but nothing approached the popularity of this one, which attempted to reassure mothers that their young sons were now in God's special care:

> Heaven's thronged with gay and careless faces,
> New-waked from dreams of dreadful things,
> They walk in green and pleasant places
> And by crystal water-springs
> Forget the nightmare field of slain,
> And the fierce thirst and the strong pain.

A SON OF ULSTER WHO DID HIS DUTY

SECOND LIEUTENANT EDWARD ALEXANDER MCCLATCHIE
ROYAL INNISKILLING FUSILIERS
DIED 10 AUGUST 1917 AGED 19
BURIED MENDINGHEM MILITARY CEMETERY

Edward McClatchie was a son of Ulster, a Protestant from Portrush, Co. Antrim. He enlisted on 4 November 1915. This means that he willingly did his duty by volunteering since conscription was not introduced until January 1916.

There is something very severe about this inscription. However, when you remember that Antrim was one of the northern Irish counties preparing armed resistance to Britain in the summer of 1914 over the British Government's preparations to introduce Home Rule for Ireland, you can imagine that the residents might have had mixed feelings about sending their sons to fight for Britain. But the Unionists were also fiercely loyal to the British crown. There must have been many conflicted families in Ireland during the First World War – like the McClatchies – on both sides of the religious divide.

WHILE THE LIGHT LASTS I SHALL REMEMBER GEORGINA

RIFLEMAN HORACE WILLIAM SMITH
KING'S ROYAL RIFLE CORPS
DIED 14 AUGUST 1917 AGED 32
BURIED ARTILLERY WOOD CEMETERY

This is a beautiful inscription, so beautiful that much of the Internet attributes it to Tennyson. But Tennyson didn't write it. It comes from *Erotion*, a poem by Algernon Swinburne (1837-1909):

> Alive, alone, without thee, with thee, dead;
> I shall remember while the light lives yet,
> And in the night-time I shall not forget.

The version in the inscription appeared in a short story by Agatha Christie, *While the Light Lasts*, which was published in 1924. Was this too late to be the source of an inscription? Not necessarily, many of the cemeteries were not finalised until late into the 1920s.

In the story, Tim Nugent was killed in East Africa during the First World War and his widow, Daphne, remarried before discovering that her husband was still alive. Hideously disfigured, he had decided not to burden his wife by returning to her. But when they meet by chance he asks her if she will come back to him. Fatefully she hesitates, Daphne doesn't love her new husband but he is rich. Tim Nugent doesn't ask again and kills himself. Haunted by her betrayal of the man she loved, Daphne remembered the original obituary notice she'd had inserted in the newspaper: 'While the light lasts I shall remember and in the darkness I shall not forget'.

Horace Smith's wife, Georgina, chose his inscription. Horace, a newsagent, owned his own business and at the time of his death he and his wife had been married eight years.

"Our never to be forgotten Captain and leader" Company message

CAPTAIN JOHN LLEWELLYN THOMAS JONES
LONDON REGIMENT ROYAL FUSILIERS
DIED 16 AUGUST 1917 AGED 22
BURIED HOOGE CRATER CEMETERY

At 4.45 am on Thursday 16 August 1917, Captain J. Llewellyn T. Jones led his men in an attack on the German-held village of Langemarck. A brother officer later told Jones' father: 'We went over the top together ... we were under terrific fire, he was absolutely cool and collected and, in fact, joked with me as we parted'. At the end of the day his Company were informed that Jones, their 'never to be forgotten Captain and leader', was among those 'missing believed killed in action'.

On the 4 April 1917, four months before his death, Jones wrote to his father:

> I have written this letter so that, in the event of anything happening to me, I do not go under without letting you dear ones at home know how much I owe to your loving care ... You know what an undemonstrative nature mine is, but my love for you all is nevertheless strong and deep, and though I said nothing about these things before I left England, it was just because – I couldn't – my heart was too full ... One has to face the prospect of getting knocked out, as many other and better fellows than I have been. All I can say is that you do not grieve for me, because, although it may sound exceedingly quixotic, how better can one make one's exit from this world than fighting for the country which has sheltered and nurtured one all through life? War is cruel and I detest it, but since it was not possible to keep out of this without loss of prestige and perhaps worse, it behoves us to carry it on to a successful conclusion ... the thought that I may never see you dear ones again in this world brings a lump to my throat and the tears to my eyes. I trust that I shall return, but ...
>
> Quoted from *War Letters of Fallen Englishmen* edited by Laurence Housman 1930

Tyne Cot Cemetery and
Memorial to the Missing

1914 - Here are recorded the
names of officers and men
of the armies of the British
Empire who fell in Ypres Salient,
but to whom the fortune of
war denied the known and
honoured burial given to their
comrades in death - 1918

Born at Kobe, Japan 9th October 1890 Sacrificed to the fallacy That war can end war

SECOND LIEUTENANT ARTHUR CONWAY YOUNG
ROYAL IRISH FUSILIERS
DIED 16 AUGUST 1917 AGED 26
BURIED TYNE COT CEMETERY

This is a very famous inscription but is it how the casualty would like to be remembered? Arthur Conway Young was the son of Robert Young, editor of the *Japan Chronicle*. Robert was an atheist, a republican and a fierce pacifist. Despite this, all three of his sons joined the war effort: Arthur as an officer in the Royal Irish Fusiliers, Douglas George as a captain in the Royal Flying Corps and Eric Andrew as a corporal despatch rider. Not that Robert Young chose his son's inscription, it was his brother, Arthur's uncle, G Young Esq, who signed for it, Robert was dead.
We know little of Arthur Young except for a letter he wrote to his father's sister, Margaret, in September 1916 in which he spoke of the horror of seeing men blown to bits, writhing in pain, running round gibbering, raving mad and telling her:

> You read no end of twaddle in the papers at home about the spirit in which men go into action ... It's rubbish like this which makes thousands of people in England think war is a great sport. As a famous Yankee general said, "War is hell", and you have only to be in the Somme one single day to know it.

And yet, this is how he went on to describe the Irish attack at Ginchy on 15 September:

> By this time we were wildly excited. Our shouts and yells alone must have struck terror into the Huns, who were firing their machine guns down the slope. But there was no wavering in the Irish host ... The numbing dread had now left me completely. Like the others I was intoxicated with the glory of it all. I can remember shouting and bawling to the men of my platoon, who were only too eager to go on.

Young concluded by telling his aunt, the attack 'will never be forgotten by those who took part in it, for it is an event we shall remember with pride to the end of our days'.

Hooge Crater Cemetery

TENDER BUT FEARLESS GENEROUS AND CHIVALROUS

SECOND LIEUTENANT ARTHUR FRANCIS DEANE
MACHINE GUN CORPS
DIED 16 AUGUST 1917 AGED 27
BURIED BEDFORD HOUSE CEMETERY

Arthur Deane's father, Henry Deane, has attributed to his son the essential qualities of a perfect Christian knight, qualities that appear to have been rather lacking in his own life. Henry Deane was not his real name, it was Henry Pockett, and in 1896 Henry was sentenced to six months imprisonment and fined £500 for 'obtaining money by false pretences from persons who wanted to borrow money from him'. In his defence, Pockett said that he "had only followed the practice of other money-lenders" and appealed for leniency. But the judge said that Pockett had shown no sign of leniency to his victims, "and the majority of the applicants were people of the poorer classes who could ill afford to part with it [their money]". At the time of his father's imprisonment Arthur Deane was six. His mother died the following year, at which point the family appear to have changed their name from Pockett to Deane. In the 1911 census, Henry Deane stated that he had been married for nine years to Florence Elizabeth Pockett and to have one eight-year-old child from the marriage. The records show that he didn't marry Florence until 1917. Arthur Deane was working in Shanghai for Messrs Butterfield and Swire when the war broke out. He returned to Britain and enlisted in September 1916. Gazetted Second Lieutenant in the Machine Gun Corps in January 1917, he was killed on the opening day of the Battle of Langemarck when the war diary recorded:

> Two guns with 1st Londons on left got well forward and covered the advance from J.8b.1.6. 2/Lt Deane was with these guns which did excellent work and found many targets on the opposite side of the valley at ranges from 600 yards to 1500 yards. One of the guns was destroyed by shell fire and the greater part of the team became casualties.

Deane's body was discovered in an unmarked grave at map reference J.7.b.81.09 on 30 April 1921. He was identified by his 'damaged discs and clothing'.

A GOOD SON
A GOOD SOLDIER
A GOOD SPORTSMAN
UNSELFISH TO THE END

CAPTAIN CECIL RICHARD LANGHAM
ROYAL SUSSEX REGIMENT
DIED 16 AUGUST 1917 AGED 26
BURIED VLAMERTINGHE NEW MILITARY CEMETERY

A father chose this inscription for his son; a father who was the Commanding Officer of the regiment in which his son served. The regiment was the 5th (Cinque Ports) Battalion Royal Sussex Regiment with which the Langham family had been associated for many years. Captain Cecil Langham was killed at Langemarck whilst attempting to bring in his badly wounded orderly. The regimental gazette recorded the impact: 'The loss of such a fine officer as Captain Langham ... was keenly felt by the whole battalion, which made their beloved C.O.'s grief their own'.

Cecil Langham joined the 5th Battalion on leaving school in 1910. As with all territorials, his peacetime commitment was limited to four years' service, regular drills and between eight to fifteen days annual training a year. This meant he was able to combine his service with a degree at Trinity Hall, Cambridge, to which he had won an open Classics scholarship. Whilst at Cambridge he rowed for both his College and for the University.

In 1914, Langham took a position with the trading house of Patterson, Simmons & Co in Singapore. He had scarcely arrived before war was declared. He applied to be released and returned to England to re-join his battalion. He served continuously on the Western Front until his death – earning from his father the approving tribute of his inscription.

United with his father & fallen brother Bert My all gone

PRIVATE ERNEST LUCAS
LANCASHIRE FUILIERS
DIED 17 AUGUST 1917 AGED 21
BRANDHOEK NEW MILITARY CEMETERY NO. 3

Mr and Mrs Albert Francis Lucas had two children, two sons, Albert born in 1894 and Ernest in 1897. Albert enlisted on 9 September 1914, went to France on 7 November 1915 serving with the 19th Battalion Manchester Regiment. He was killed in action on 1 July 1916, the first day of the Somme Campaign. His body was never found so he had no grave but is commemorated on the Thiepval Memorial.

Ernest served with the 11th Battalion Lancashire Fusiliers. He died of wounds at a Casualty Clearing Station at Brandhoek on 17 August 1917. Both Ernest and Albert were unmarried. Their father, a merchant shippers' clerk, died on 5 April 1920 aged 57. By the time his wife, Mrs Sarah Lucas, was asked for Ernest's personal inscription her family was dead – 'My all gone'.

Thank God: we know that he "batted well" in the last great game of all

SECOND LIEUTENANT RICHARD DOUGLAS MILES MC
ROYAL IRISH FUSILIERS
DIED 17 AUGUST 1917 AGED 27
BURIED BRANDHOEK NEW MILITARY CEMETERY NO.3

This inscription comes from the last lines of *The Fool*, a poem by the Anglo-Canadian author Robert William Service. The fool, so-called by his parent, is Dick, a young boy who insists on leaving school to join the army. Dick is killed:

> Dick with his rapture of song and sun,
> Dick of the yellow hair,
> Dicky whose life had just begun,
> Carrion-cold out there,

The parent is both grief stricken and mortified:

> And I called him a fool ... oh how blind was I!
> And the cup of my grief's abrim.

But finds comfort in the fact that:

> Thank God! we know that he "Batted well"
> In the last great Game of all.

With an MC to his credit Richard Douglas Miles had certainly 'batted well', the sporting analogy reminiscent of the schoolboy who rallied the ranks with his cry, 'Play up, play up and play the game' in Henry Newbolt's famous but subsequently derided poem, *Vitae Lampada*. Miles, born in Jamaica where his father was the Collector General, was wounded in the Irish Fusiliers' attack at Langemarck on 16 August and died the next day.

I HAVE FOUGHT THE GOOD FIGHT I HAVE FINISHED MY COURSE I HAVE KEPT THE FAITH

SECOND LIEUTENANT WALTER MORSE JOTCHAM
WORCESTERSHIRE REGIMENT
DIED 19 AUGUST 1917 AGED 28
BURIED NEW IRISH FARM CEMETERY

There are five Jotchams on the Wootton-under-Edge war memorial, Walter, his brother Cyril, and three of their cousins: Herbert, William and Fred. Walter and Cyril share a marble memorial plaque in St Mary's Church. This records their dates of death and concludes with the same quotation as that on Walter's headstone: I have fought a good fight, I have finished my course, I have kept the faith.

The words come from the Second Epistle of Paul the Apostle to Timothy. Paul, acknowledging that 'the time of my departure is at hand', his martyrdom, looks forward to the 'crown of righteousness, which the Lord, the righteous judge, shall give me at that day'. It is the same crown of righteousness that will be awarded to all those who have endured suffering and faced death for Christ's sake – as, in their parents' opinion, both Walter and Cyril Jotcham had done.

Walter had gone to America in June 1914 and settled in Washington State as a fruit farmer. However, soon after the outbreak of war he enlisted in the Canadian Expeditionary Force and returned to Europe. He saw action on the Western Front from August 1915 until July 1916 when he returned to England to take up a commission in the Worcestershire Regiment. Back in France in March 1917, he was killed on the night of the 18/19 August leading his platoon across the Steenbeek in the face of fierce German fire.

His brother, Cyril, joined the Gloucestershire Yeomanry in January 1915. He served with them in in Egypt and Gallipoli, from where he was invalided home with dysentery. He returned in May 1916 to serve with them in Palestine and died there of malaria on 16 June 1918. He is buried in Kantara War Memorial Cemetery. His headstone inscription comes from John Bunyan's *Pilgrim's Progress*:

> And he passed over
> And all the trumpets sounded
> For him on the other side

A NOBLE TYPE OF GOOD HEROIC WOMANHOOD

STAFF NURSE NELLIE SPINDLER
QUEEN ALEXANDRA'S IMPERIAL NURSING SERVICE
DIED 21 AUGUST 1917 AGED 26
BURIED LIJSSENTHOEK MILITARY CEMETERY

> *Leeds Mercury* Tuesday 28 August 1917
> LEEDS NURSE KILLED BY THE HUNS
> Victim of Bombardment in France
> Miss Nellie Spindler, who, from 1912 to 1915, was a nurse at the Leeds Township Infirmary, was killed in France on August 21st by a German shell during the bombardment on a stationary hospital where she was engaged. She was 26 years of age, and was a daughter of the Chief Inspector of Police at Stanley Road, Wakefield. In November 1915, she left Leeds to take up duties as nurse at a military hospital in Staffordshire, where she remained until last June, when she proceeded to France.

The following day's *Leeds Mercury* published further particulars of Nurse Spindler's death under the headline – THE MURDERED NURSE.

> A letter has been received from Miss M. Wood, sister-in-charge of the hospital who states:- "Your daughter became unconscious immediately she was hit, and she passed away perfectly peacefully at 11.30 a.m. - just 20 minutes afterwards. I was with her at the time; but after the first minute or two she did not know me. It was a great mercy she was oblivious to her surroundings, for the shells continued to fall in for the rest of the day."

Nellie Spindler's mother chose her inscription; it comes from *Santa Filomena*, 1857, Henry Wadsworth Longfellow's tribute to Florence Nightingale:

> A lady with a lamp shall stand
> In the great history of the land,
> A noble type of good,
> Heroic womanhood.

Their bodies Are buried in peace But their name Liveth for evermore

SECOND LIEUTENANT DONALD LYLE WHITMARSH
HAMPSHIRE REGIMENT
DIED 22 AUGUST 1917 AGED 32
BURIED TYNE COT CEMETERY

'Their name liveth for evermore', Ecclesiasticus 44:14, are the words on the Stone of Remembrance; there is one in every War Graves Commission cemetery with more than 1,000 burials. Designed in a deliberately abstract style in order to appeal to people of 'all faiths and none', Edwin Lutyens outlined his ideas for this 'great stone' in a letter he wrote to Fabian Ware, newly appointed Chairman of the Imperial War Graves Commission, in April 1917:

> On platforms made of not less than 3 steps the upper and the lower steps of a width twice that of the centre step: to give due dignity: place one great stone of fine proportion 12 feet long set fair and finely wrot – without due ornament and trickery and elaborate carvings and inscribe thereon one thought in clear letters so that all men for all time may read and know the reason these stones are so placed throughout France ...

The 'one thought in clear letters' was chosen by Rudyard Kipling – Their name liveth for evermore. The 'clear letters' were the work of Macdonald Gill who was responsible for designing the special lettering that the Commission use to this day. Lutyens suggested 39 different names for his stone – Stone of Remembrance was not one of them.

'Their name liveth for evermore' was carefully chosen. The whole verse reads: 'Their bodies are buried in peace; but their name liveth for evermore'. To be acceptable to people of 'all faiths' the first six words had to be omitted to avoid offending Hindus who cremate their dead. Whitmarsh's inscription quotes the whole verse. His brother-in-law, his sister's husband, chose it. Whitmarsh's parents appear to have been alive but the family had fragmented in 1887 when his mother confessed that her two youngest children – of whom Donald was one – were not her husband's but her lover's. After the divorce, salaciously reported in all the newspapers, Mrs Whitmarsh went to New Zealand. Donald was brought up by his father's sister.

Tyne Cot
Cemetery

WHO DIES IF ENGLAND LIVES
WHO LIVES IF ENGLAND DIES

MAJOR HENRY FRANCIS FARQUHARSON MURRAY
BLACK WATCH
DIED 23 AUGUST 1917 AGED 36
BURIED BRANDHOEK NEW MILITARY CEMETERY NO. 3

> At 11 a.m. nothing less than a tragedy to the Battalion occurred. The Commanding Officer, Major H.F.F. Murray, temporarily in command owing to Lieutenant Colonel Innes having been ordered not to take part in the attack, on account of the necessity for keeping at least one senior officer to replace a possible casualty, had made his headquarters in a captured German concrete dug-out. Unfortunately the entrance faced the enemy, and a shell entered it, killing 12 of the Battalion Headquarters Staff and wounding nine others, among the former being Major Murray ...
>
> *History of the Black Watch in the Great War 1914-1918* Volume III

Major Murray's fate was the result of previous success, the German dug-out had been captured by the British but its entrance now faced the wrong way making it vulnerable to its previous owners' shells.

Henry Murray's wife, Madeline, chose his inscription. The line, 'Who dies if England live' comes from the last verse of *For All We Have and Are*, the poem Rudyard Kipling wrote in September 1914 in response to the outbreak of war, which ends:

What stands if Freedom fall?
Who dies if England live?

Although the second line of the inscription is close to Kipling's it is not the same. Murray's inscription, as written, forms the final frame of an official 1916 film showing preparations for the Battle of the Somme, *Sons of Empire Episode 4*. This is what gave the words prominence. As a postscript to this, it is interesting to see how the sentiments of Kipling's poem and Murray's inscription were common to both sides. In 1914 the German poet Heinrich Lersch published his own poetic response to the outbreak of war, *Soldaten Abschied*, the Soldiers' Farewell. Each of the five verses ends with the same words – 'Deutschland muss leben, und wenn wir sterben mussen', Germany must live even if we must die.

DIED AT THE GUNS HEARTENING HIS MEN AT ZILLEBEKE LAKE

CAPTAIN JOHN LINDSAY KELSALL
ROYAL FIELD ARTILLERY
DIED 28 AUGUST 1917 AGED 26
BURIED THE HUTS CEMETERY

One of an officer's main duties was to look after his men, to maintain their morale. This was done both by winning their respect and by discipline. The little book, *A General's Letters to His Son on Obtaining His Commission*, published in 1917, offers the following advice:

> Your men will obey you because you are their officer, but you will succeed in getting infinitely more out of them if you can win their love and respect. Let your Platoon always be your first care. Put yourself in the position of your men, and never ask them to do what you would not be ready to do yourself in like circumstances.
>
> In a disciplined company when the Captain has given the word to advance, the individual obeys, certain that whether he advances or not his comrades on either side will do so, and whatever his own feelings may be, he cannot but obey. Having done so, and believing himself a hero among a band of heroes, he acquires the courage which comes from discipline, and becomes a brave man though he was not born one.

Zillebeke was already an appalling and dangerous place to be in August 1917 before 34.9 mm of rain fell over the 26th and 27th of the month. Keeping the guns firing became a herculean task, not made any easier by the fact that the Germans had the range of the British guns and kept up a constant bombardment.

The *Rochdale Observor* announced Kelsall's death in their 5 September edition; his family were partners in the Rochdale firm of Kelsall and Kemp, big employers in the town, which did good business during the war making khaki cloth for the army. After recounting the details of his education and army service it finished its report with the words: 'He was popular, loved and respected alike by officers and men'.

Tranquil you lie ... Your memory hallowed In the land you loved

LIEUTENANT RICHARD CHESTER CHESTER-MASTER DSO & BAR
KING'S ROYAL RIFLE CORPS
DIED 30 AUGUST 1917 AGED 47
BURIED LOCRE HOSPICE CEMETERY

Lt. Colonel Chester-Master's inscription comes from the first verse of the once very popular Remembrance hymn, O Valiant Hearts, written by Sir John Arkwright in 1917.

> O valiant hearts who to your glory came
> Through clouds of conflict and through battle flame;
> Tranquil you lie, your knightly virtue proved,
> Your memory hallowed in the land you loved.

Chester-Master was a professional soldier. He had served in the South African War but in 1914, on the reserve list, was Chief Constable of Gloucestershire. He re-joined his regiment on the outbreak of war, went with it to France and was shot by a sniper on 30 August 1917. Chester-Master's DSO and Bar bear testament to his qualities as a soldier, and the tribute the Acting Chief Constable, distributed to all the police stations in Gloucestershire, bears testament to his qualities as a man:

> In him the country has lost a brave and experienced soldier; the county of Gloucestershire has lost a valued and high-minded official; the Police Force has lost a head who had devoted the best energies of his life, since he became Chief Constable, to their official and private welfare; and a great many people have lost a friend whom they had learnt to honour and love. He has passed away in the midst of what promised to be a brilliant military career, leaving behind him a memory which will never be forgotten of a 'gallant gentleman' in the best and noblest sense of the word.

Richard Chester-Master's wife, Geraldine, chose his inscription. Born Geraldine Mary Rose Arkwright, she was Sir John Arkwright's sister.

Locre Hospice Cemetery

In loving memory of Jim & his four brothers killed in action united in death

PRIVATE JAMES FRIEND SHAW
LONDON REGIMENT
DIED 31 AUGUST 1917 AGED 20
BURIED MENDINGHEM MILITARY CEMETERY

James Shaw was one of six brothers, five of whom were killed in the war. Jesse Shaw, the fourth brother, who had emigrated to Australia, was the first to die. He enlisted on 4 September 1914 and was wounded at Gallipoli on 30 April 1915 with a bullet in his right lung. He died on a hospital ship three days later, 3 May, and was buried at sea. He is commemorated on the Lone Pine Memorial.

Henry Shaw, the second brother, was killed in action on 15 September 1916. His body was never identified and he is commemorated on the Thiepval Memorial. The next two brothers, Thomas and Edward were both killed on the same day, 3 May 1917, two years to the day after Jesse died. Neither of their bodies were found; Thomas, a private in the King's Royal Rifle Corps is commemorated on the Arras Memorial, Edward, a Lieutenant in the Australian Infantry, on the Villers-Bretonneux Memorial. James died of wounds three months later. He is the only brother to have a grave and therefore an inscription. This was chosen by the boys' father, Thomas, their mother, Harriet, having died sometime before 1911.

Many people know of the five Beechey brothers who were killed in the war, and the five Souls brothers, but the five Shaw brothers had never been identified until Yvonne Fenter did the research for the Imperial War Museum's *Lives of the First World War*.

After one crowded hour Of glorious life He sleeps well

PRIVATE JOHN WILSON KELSO
SEAFORTH HIGHLANDERS
DIED 2 SEPTEMBER 1917 AGED 19
BURIED VLAMERTINGHE NEW MILITARY CEMETERY

William Wilson Kelso created his son's inscription, combining a line from Shakespeare's *Macbeth* with a phrase from the *The Call*, a very short poem by Thomas Osbert Mordaunt (1730-1809):

> Sound, sound the clarion, fill the fife,
> To all the sensual world proclaim
> One crowded hour of glorious life
> Is worth an age without a name.

Kelso served with the 6th Battalion Seaforth Highlanders, part of the 51st Highland Division, which went into the trenches at Langemarck on 20 August and remained in the area until 20 September. The History of the 51st Division remarks that this was an interesting period on three counts: 'First the mud ... the ground throughout the whole front was so sodden with rain and churned up by shell-fire as to be impossible to troops in any numbers'. Second was the 'consistently lavish use of the recently-introduced mustard gas, which caused numerous cases of slightly-gassed men, and a lesser number of men seriously gassed. The latter suffered indescribable agonies, and either ultimately died or made an insufficient recovery ever to return to the ranks as whole men'. The third feature was the aerial bombing, which the Germans had begun to use increasingly at this time. The bombing was 'difficult to deal with, as shelters for the men could not be provided by means of dug-outs in the clay soil of Flanders'.

Kelso died of wounds at a Field Ambulance on 2 September, whether from gas, mud, shell or bomb it hasn't been possible to tell.

> After life's fitful fever he sleeps well;
> Treason has done his worst: nor steel, nor poison,
> Malice domestic, foreign levy, nothing,
> Can touch him further.
>
> *Macbeth* Act III Scene ii William Shakespeare

On honour's scroll His name shall be Though all unknown to history

LIEUTENANT WILFRED STUART LANE PAYNE, MC
ROYAL GARRISON ARTILLERY ATTACHED ROYAL FLYING CORPS
DIED 4 SEPTEMBER 1917 AGED 24
BURIED MENDINGHEM BRITISH CEMETERY

It would surprise Mr RH Payne, who chose this inscription, to learn how much his brother Wilfred is not unknown to history – thanks to the Internet. A UK Incoming Passenger List shows that Payne sailed from Valparaiso, Chile, and arrived in Liverpool on 5 September 1915. The digitized *London Gazette* shows that he was gazetted Second Lieutenant in the Royal Garrison Artillery six days later, on 11 September 1915. The 3 March 1917 edition gives the citation for his Military Cross:

> For conspicuous gallantry in action: he displayed great courage and skill when employed as Observation Officer. Later he rescued six men who had been buried in a dug-out.

The Commonwealth War Graves Commission website gives his rank, age, previous service with the Royal Garrison Artillery, parents – Charles and Anna Lucy Payne of British Guiana – and his place of burial. Further CWGC documents show that he was attached to No. 7 Squadron and that it was his brother, Mr RH Payne, Plantation Wales, West Bank Demerara River, British Guiana, who chose his inscription.

Payne was the observer in an RE. 8 (a reconnaissance bomber based at Proven) piloted by Thomas Ernest Wray. They were shot down at 08:25 hours north of Ypres, the 14th 'victory' of the German flying ace, Rudolf Berthold, who went on to have a total of 44 victories, 16 of them after his right arm had been paralysed by a bullet.

Payne and nineteen-year-old Wray, are buried in adjacent graves.

That from this Great big world You've chosen me

SECOND LIEUTENANT REGINALD OTTO WEBER
THE LOYAL NORTH LANCASHIRE REGIMENT
DIED 5 SEPTEMBER 1917 AGED 25
BURIED LIJSSENTHOEK MILITARY CEMETERY

The words may sound as though they come from a revivalist hymn but they don't, they come from a love duet, *They Wouldn't Believe Me*, written in 1914 by the American composer Jerome Kern for the musical, *The Girl From Utah*. The song became a massive 'hit' and made Kern's reputation. This is the relevant verse:

And when I tell them,
And I certainly am going to tell them,
That I'm the man whose wife one day you'll be
They'll never believe me, they'll never believe me,
That from this great big world you've chosen me

Reginald Otto Weber was the youngest son of Frederick Weber, a wealthy German-born fur trader living in London, who signed for his son's inscription. It's difficult to imagine what Frederick Weber meant by it, other than that death chose his son from a cast of thousands.

Weber served with the 3rd Battalion the Loyal North Lancashire Regiment but was attached to the 8th at the time of his death. The battalion went into the front line on 30 August 1917 and remained there until the 5th September, during which time the regimental history recorded the death of Weber and eight soldiers. According to the records of No. 17 Casualty Clearing Station, Lijssenthoek, Weber died of wounds – 'gunshot wounds to spine'.

By chance there is one other casualty with the surname Weber buried in Lijssthenthoek Military Cemetery – Gefreiter Karl Weber of the German army.

HE DID HIS BIT

PRIVATE ROBERT THOMPSON
LABOUR CORPS
DIED 9 SEPTEMBER 1917 AGED 22
BURIED DOZINGHEM MILITARY CEMETERY

If you think this sounds rather a begrudging epitaph then you wouldn't be alone, but you would be wrong. To do your bit was a popular way of saying that you were doing your duty by your country; you were doing your bit.

At the beginning of Ian Hay's semi-fictional 1915 novel, *The First Hundred Thousand*, written with typical British self-deprecation and understatement about the experiences of the earliest volunteers, there's a poem which must have summarised how many soldiers felt about the war: yes they've given up their jobs but no they haven't done it for glory rather just, 'To have a slap at Kaiser Bill'. And as they go off to war they know that some of them will not come back:

> But all we ask, if that befall,
> Is this, within your hearts be writ
> This single-line memorial: –
> He did his duty – and his bit!

Robert Thompson did his bit. Originally Private Thompson 25296 of the East Yorkshire Regiment, he was serving with the 22nd Company Labour Corps when he died from the effects of gas in a Casualty Clearing Station at Dozinghem. His transfer from the East Yorkshire Regiment to the Labour Corps suggests that he was no longer deemed fit for front line service, possibly as a result of having been wounded. Nevertheless, the work done by the Corps was still dangerous work and still within the reach of the guns – and the gas.

CHA TILL GU BRATH GU LA NA CRUINNE

PRIVATE ALEXANDER MCCRIMMON
AUSTRALIAN INFANTRY
DIED 16 SEPTEMBER 1917 AGED 46
BURIED HOOGE CRATER CEMETERY

The Gaelic translates as, 'He will not return until the great day of doom and burning', the Day of Judgement. The lines come from the chorus of *MacCrimmon's Lament*, the lament for a piper from the Isle of Skye who was killed in the 1745 rebellion.

No more, no more, no more returning,
In peace nor in war is he returning;
Till dawns the great day of doom and burning,
MacCrimmon is home no more returning.

Alexander McCrimmon was born in Skye in 1871. This is not to say that he was related to the MacCrimmons of the lament, who had been hereditary pipers to the Clan MacCleod for three hundred years, but nor is there anything to say that he wasn't. In 1910, aged 39, he emigrated to Australia. Seven years later, McCrimmon enlisted in the Australian Infantry and by May 1917 was in France. His battalion went into the trenches on 16 September and he was killed that day.

MacCrimmon is a haunting figure in Scottish legend, a ghostly figure who accompanies men into battle:

And there in the front of the men were marching
With feet that made no mark,
The old grey ghosts of the ancient fighters
Come back again from the dark;
And in front of them all MacCrimmon piping
A weary tune and sore,
"On gathering day, for ever and ever,
MacCrimmon comes no more".

Cha Till Maccruimein (MacCrimmon Will Never Return) E A Mackintosh 1893-1917

MY FIRST PRIDE MY FIRST JOY MY BRAVE SOLDIER BOY

PRIVATE HEREWARD WILLIAM RAY
AUSTRALIAN INFANTRY
DIED 18 SEPTEMBER 1917 AGED 24
BURIED HOOGE CRATER CEMETERY

Hereward Ray was his mother's eldest child – 'her first pride, her first joy'. He was also 'her brave soldier boy'. Do the words intentionally echo a popular American anti-war song, written in 1915? If this echo was intentional then Mrs Ray was rebuking the song-writers, not agreeing with them. This is the chorus of the song:

I didn't raise my boy to be a soldier,
I brought him up to be my pride and joy.
Who dares to place a musket on his shoulder,
To shoot some other mother's darling boy?
Let nations arbitrate their future troubles,
It's time to lay the sword and gun away.
There'd be no war today,
If mothers all would say,
"I didn't raise my boy to be a soldier."

The Ray family was committed to the war. There was no conscription in Australia but Hereward Ray's stepfather and brother both fought, as did his mother's brother, Hector Archibald Maclean, who was killed in action on 9 June 1916, aged 47. Two of his cousins also served, one was killed and the other, invalided home, died of wounds in Australia.
Hereward Ray enlisted in March 1915 and served with the 22nd Australian Infantry in Gallipoli and France, where it took part in the Battle of Pozieres. Early in 1917 it went to Flanders. Ray was killed in the trenches on 18 September 1917. A witness related how Ray and Sergeant Kelly died of head injuries having been hit by a shell at Jabber Trench, Westhoek.

"I LEAVE MYSELF IN GOD'S HANDS" EXTRACT FROM HIS DIARY WRITTEN 19.9.17

LIEUTENANT JAMES LUNAN
GORDON HIGHLANDERS
DIED 20 SEPTEMBER 1917
BURIED POELCAPELLE BRITISH CEMETERY

Written the day before his death, the diary entry indicates that James Lunan knew how the odds were stacked. The next day, 20 September, he was to lead his men in an attack on the German lines on the opening day of the Battle of Menin Road. Attacking across a 14,500 yard front, the British achieved their objectives, showing this time what could be done in good weather and with a well-prepared attack. But James Lunan had been killed – as he obviously suspected he might be, his body not discovered until three years later. Lunan's faith in God was no temporary eve-of-battle phenomenon. As the *Aberdeen Press and Journal* of 28 September reported, he had been an active member of the Boys Brigade connected with his church, Skene Street Congregational Church, where he was also secretary of the Sunday School. Lunan came from a professional Aberdeen family. He had been educated at Aberdeen Grammar School and Robert Gordon College and he worked at The North of Scotland and Town and County Bank Ltd. A member of the Territorial Force, he was called up on the outbreak of war, served on the Western Front from February 1915, achieved the rank of sergeant and then in December 1915 was commissioned into the Gordon Highlanders.

Forget me not dear land for which I fell

CAPTAIN OWEN ROBERT LLOYD MC
KING'S SHROPSHIRE LIGHT INFANTRY
DIED 20 SEPTEMBER 1917 AGED 25
BURIED CEMENT HOUSE CEMETERY

The Times, 5 October 1917
"He was a very gallant soldier and an exceptionally fine leader of men. We attacked on the 20th ... Captain Lloyd saw the attack developing on his right, and got up and led his company on, and it was as he was doing so that he fell, hit by two bullets. The ground was open and raked by machine gun fire ... The men of his company, at the risk of their lives, went to your son, bandaged him up, and took him to the aid post. He died there, after thanking the men who took him down ... I liked him personally so much. I think he would rather have died that way than any other."

Letter from Lloyd's Colonel

Owen Lloyd's father chose his inscription, adapting a line from Joseph Lee's, *Our British Dead*, first published in the *Spectator* in January 1917. The poem opens with a quote from Simonides:
'O stranger, bring the Spartans word, that here, obedient to their command we lie'. Lloyd's inscription comes from the second verse:

Forget us not, O Land for which we fell –
May it go well with England, still go well.
Keep her bright banners without blot or stain,
Lest we should dream that we have died in vain.
Brave be the days to come, when we
Are but a wistful memory ...
Here do we lie, dead but not discontent,
That which we found to do has had accomplishment.

Simonides' dead ask that their country is told they have done what was asked of them; Lee's dead, who have also done what was asked of them, want to feel that the country they have died for will be worthy of their deaths, 'Lest we should dream that we have died in vain'.

I AM HERE AS THE RESULT OF UNCIVILISED NATIONS

CORPORAL JOHN COLLIN GOODALL
AUSTRALIAN INFANTRY
DIED 20 SEPTEMBER 1917 AGED 20
BURIED NEW IRISH FARM CEMETERY

Whilst allowing next-of-kin the right to choose a sixty-six-character inscription, the Imperial War Graves Commission reserved the right to censor ones they considered plainly unsuitable. Questionable inscriptions would be referred to the Committee. In July 1922 the Vice-Chairman referred an inscription which read: 'He died the just for the unjust'. The minutes record: 'The Commission agreed to the inscription being refused'. Over a year later he submitted another inscription of a very similar hue: 'I am here as a result of uncivilised nations'. This time the minutes say: 'After some discussion the Commission agreed that this inscription might be accepted'. This is Corporal Goodall's inscription, the indefinite article being changed for the definite on the actual headstone.

Don't both inscriptions have the same ambiguity? Who are the 'unjust', who are the 'uncivilised nations'? Do both 'unjust' and 'uncivilised' refer to the Germans? In which case, why should one inscription have been allowed and the other refused?

John Collin Goodall, a bicycle maker from Brisbane, enlisted on 4 April 1915 at the age of 18. He served in Gallipoli until the evacuation and was then posted to France where he was severely wounded and spent six months in hospital. He was killed in action on 20 September 1917. According to witnesses:

> Goodall was sniped, being shot between the eyes and killed instantly ... I saw his body and examined him. He was my mate and I never heard what happened to his body afterwards.

> He was shot through the head by a sniper just as we were on the point of reaching our objective. He was just in front of me at Glencorse Wood. He had to be left there.

And it was 'there', at map reference J.8.b.5.5., that Goddall's body was discovered in April 1921 and buried in New Irish Farm Cemetery where 3,271 out of the 4,719 burials are unidentified.

JUST FOR A SCRAP OF PAPER

GUNNER THOMAS HENRY BRINDLEY
ROYAL FIELD ARTILLERY
20 SEPTEMBER 1917 AGED 20
BURIED POND FARM CEMETERY

On 19 April 1839 Britain and the German Confederation were among the signatories of the Treaty of London, guaranteeing the independence and neutrality of Belgium. On 31 July 1914 the King of Belgium reminded the signatories of their obligation. Germany ignored it and on 3 August 1914 invaded France through Belgium, leading Britain to declare war on Germany the next day. The German Chancellor, Bethmann-Hollweg, was reported to have been incredulous at the idea that Britain would go to war over 'a scrap of paper'. The remark gave Britain a source of propaganda; a recruiting poster was produced showing the signatures on the 1839 document under the heading, 'The Scrap of Paper' with the appeal, 'The Germans have broken their pledged word and devastated Belgium. Help keep your country's honour bright by restoring Belgium her liberty'.
Brindley, who at the age of 13 was an errand boy, joined up in April 1916 and served with "C" Battery, 124th Brigade RFA. He was killed on the opening day of the Battle of Menin Road. His family kept a letter from the Brigade Chaplain who wrote to tell them:

> Your son .... was killed in action this morning. He was in the gun pit at the time when a shell landed right on top of the pit, wounding him in the head, stomach and a compound fracture of the right leg. He was so seriously wounded that from the first there was little or no hope of his recovery.. He was at once removed to the nearest Advanced Dressing Station where all that could be done for him was done and from there he was sent off in an ambulance to the Main Dressing Station but his soul passed away before reaching there. His body was reverently laid to rest this afternoon in the little British military cemetery at 'Pond Farm' which is just outside the ruined village of Kemmel on the borders of France and Belgium.

... Just for a scrap of paper ...

Leaving a widow and three children his duty done

PRIVATE HAROLD ST CLAIR HENSTRIDGE
AUSTRALIAN MACHINE GUN CORPS
DIED 20 SEPTEMBER 1917 AGED 30
BURIED HOOGE CRATER CEMETERY

Henstridge's three children, Kevin, Betty and Bobbie, were aged 6, 5 and 2 at the time of their father's death. Since his whole service file has been digitised, we can see that his widow, Violet, subsequently received a fortnightly pension of £2, Kevin of 20 shillings, Betty 15 shillings and Bobbie 10 shillings.

Henstridge, who described himself as an advertisement writer, enlisted on 14 August 1915, trained as a machine gunner and served with the Australian Machine Gun Corps 3rd Coy in France and Flanders. He was killed by a shell on 20 September 1917.

The witnesses to the Red Cross Enquiry Bureau give slightly contradictory accounts of what happened. The most lurid describes how, as they were advancing in open formation at Polygon Wood a shell came over and hit him:

> It was about midnight ... when it happened ... Henstridge was the only one hit. We looked for him and found pieces of fresh flesh ... I feel sure the shell wiped him out ...

Others also say that he was blown to pieces but some say that they saw his body and helped to bury it. This raises the question as to how much detail the Red Cross passed on to the next-of-kin? Who would want to know about finding pieces of their son or husband's 'fresh flesh'? However, as the letter to Mrs Henstridge is also in this file we can see that it says nothing about Henstridge being blown to pieces, only that he was killed and probably buried nearby. And this does appear to have been what happened. In March 1919, his body was discovered at map reference J.8.c.5.0. There was no cross on the grave but it did still have its identity disc, which meant that Henstridge could be buried under a named headstone. The identity disc was dispatched to Mrs Henstridge on 9 June 1920.

A BRAVE BRIGHT SPIRIT HIS LAST WORDS WERE "CARRY ON"

SECOND LIEUTENANT RONALD HOWARTH STOTT
THE LOYAL NORTH LANCASHIRE REGIMENT
DIED 20 SEPTEMBER 1917 AGED 21
BURIED KANDAHAR MILITARY CEMETERY

Stott - Killed in action on the 20th of September, 1917, Second-Lieutenant Ronald Howorth Stott, L.N. Lancashire Regiment, attached the Rifle Brigade, aged 21, the dearly loved only son of Mr. and Mrs C.H. Stott 112 Hare Street
"God grant the sacrifice be not in vain"

Rochdale Observer 29 September 1917

Mr and Mrs Stott chose a line from John Oxenham's *Epilogue 1914* for the newspaper announcement of their son's death. For his headstone inscription they quoted from *Nelson*, a poem by Gerald Massey (1828-1907), in which a sailor speaks of his admiration for his old leader but admits that when he saw Nelson at dawn on the day of Trafalgar:

His proudly-wasted face, wave-worn,
Was loftily serene;
I saw the brave, bright spirit burn
There all too plainly seen;
As though the sword this time was drawn
Forever from the sheath;
And when its work to-day was done,
All would be dark in death.

It was only three weeks since Stott had been home on leave, celebrating his 21st birthday. Had his parents seen 'death' in his face? Like all parents they must have feared the future, especially as Ronald was their only child not just their only son as the newspaper stated. The second part of the inscription, 'Carry on', is now always thought of in terms of 'Keep calm and carry on', but it is a formal military order, a command from an officer to continue with your duties. On the day he was killed, Stott was leading his men on the opening day of the Battle of Menin Road. As he died he instructed his men to 'carry on'. The *Rochdale Observor* concluded its report by saying that Stott's men brought his body back and buried it behind the lines.

Man am I grown
A man's work must I do
Else wherefore born

PRIVATE CLARENCE ROBERT FOWLE
DIED 20 SEPTEMBER 1917 AGED 18
SOUTH AFRICAN INFANTRY
BURIED BRANDHOEK NEW MILITARY CEMETERY NO. 3

Is there a personal story behind this inscription? The context suggests there might be. The inscription comes from Tennyson's *Idylls of the King*. Gareth, the youngest of his parents' sons, wants to join his brothers as a knight at Arthur's Round Table. But his mother wants to keep him safe and refuses to let him go, telling him, 'Stay my best son! ye are yet more boy than man', and trying to persuade him that he can train for manhood by following the deer, in other words by hunting in the forest. Gareth replies:

> ... O mother,
> How can ye keep me tether'd to you? – Shame.
> Man am I grown, a man's work must I do.
> Follow the deer? follow the Christ, the King,
> Live pure, speak true, right wrong, follow the King –
> Else, wherefore born?

Clarence Fowle was 18 when he was killed, technically too young to be at the front unless he had his parents' signed permission. Had he persuaded an unwilling mother to let him go? He served with the 1st South African Infantry Regiment and was killed in the attack on Frezenberg Ridge on the first day of the Battle of Menin Road. Of the 20 September 1917, John Buchan, in his *History of South African Forces in the Great War*, said, "That day's battle cracked the kernel of the German defence in the Salient. It showed only a limited advance ... but every inch of the ground was vital', however:

> Few struggles in the campaign were more desperate or carried out in a more gruesome battlefield. The mass of quagmires, splintered woods, ruined husks of pill-boxes, water-filled shell holes, and foul creeks which made up the land on both sides of the Menin road was a sight which, to the recollection of most men, must seem like a fevered nightmare. ... the elements seemed to have blended with each other to make it a limbo outside mortal experience and almost beyond human imagining.

A WILLING SACRIFICE FOR THE WORLD'S PEACE

SECOND LIEUTENANT WILLIAM KEITH SEABROOK
AUSTRALIAN INFANTRY
DIED 21 SEPTEMBER 1917 AGED 21
BURIED LIJSSENTHOEK MILITARY CEMETERY

This is a phenomenally magnanimous inscription from a mother who had three sons killed on two consecutive days: George and Theo on 20 September 1917, and William on the 21st. But to whom does the word sacrifice refer? Surely to her son, William Keith Seabrook – and by implication her other sons – since they were the ones who volunteered, who offered themselves willingly.

Mrs Seabrook instituted a Red Cross search within weeks of her son's deaths, but it was never easy to find out exactly what had happened to one person, let alone three. Some reports say that a single shell killed all three brothers, but others give more convincing accounts, like Private Cooper's:

> T.L. Seabrook was killed by the same shell that wounded me, in fact I fell across him when I was hit. He was killed instantaneously. We were in a trench just this side of Polygon Wood, it was about 9 am.

Private Arnold gives slightly more gruesome details:

> Hit by shell head and stomach and legs. Died very soon after. He was badly hit. I saw him hit. Don't know whether he was buried. He was a friend of mine.

Private Marshall gives a sequence to the brother's deaths since it was whilst he was talking to George Seabrook that he:

> pointed out his brother Theo Leslie Seabrook's body lying on the ground. He had been killed by a shell. Informant states that another brother, Second Lieutenant William Keith Seabrook had been killed still earlier in the day, and that the Lieutenant had been his officer.

George was killed soon afterwards but William Seabrook, although wounded, didn't die until the next day. After his death a photograph of his gentle-faced mother was found in his pocket. It has a bullet hole through the bottom left-hand corner.

Lijssenthoek Military Cemetery

An Ideal Soldier and Very Perfect Gentleman Beloved by All His Men

BRIGADIER GENERAL FRANCIS AYLMER MAXWELL VC CSI DSO
GENERAL STAFF
DIED 21 SEPTEMBER 1917 AGED 46
BURIED YPRES RESERVOIR CEMETERY

There's a plaque in St Giles' Cathedral, Edinburgh that reads:

> Brigadier General Francis Aylmer Maxwell VC, CSI, DSO
> Killed in action at Ypres 21 September 1917
> A gallant soldier and very perfect gentleman beloved by all his men.
> A tribute from the officers, NCOs & men 27th Inf. Bde.
> 9th (Scottish) Division

General Maxwell's widow quoted from this plaque when the time came for her to choose an inscription for his headstone, just changing one word – Charlotte Maxwell described her husband as an ideal soldier rather than a 'gallant' one.

'Beloved by all his men', how true can this be? Maxwell had a reputation as a martinet but when Lieutenant Archibald Gordon MacGregor, who had served under Maxwell in the 27th Infantry Brigade, came to write a memoir for his grandchildren in the 1960s he could say of Maxwell that he was universally admired and immensely popular.

> Maxwell, 46 years old, was a smallish man of slight build but of tremendous personality, and utterly fearless ... Not infrequently he did not hesitate to challenge or even disobey orders from superiors, if he thought such orders were ill-advised ... Maxwell's death at Ypres in Sept. 1917 was due to a disregard of danger that amounted to foolhardiness. He was killed in no-mans-land after exposing himself to a German sniper who had missed him with his first shot. But had he not constantly risked his life he would not have been the wonderful leader of men that he was.
>
> *War Diary 1917-1919 Written for his Grandchildren*
> www.AnnaWelti.com/archie.asp

When the fields are white with daisies I'll return In loving memory

PRIVATE GEORGE EDWARD BEAVIS
AUSTRALIAN INFANTRY
DIED 21 SEPTEMBER 1917 AGED 20
BURIED THE HUTS CEMETERY

George Beavis' inscription comes from a popular Irish song written towards the end of the nineteenth century. The words originally referred to a sailor but Bamforth changed them to 'soldier' for a set of their sentimental First World War picture postcards:

> I once stood in a harbour, as a ship was going out,
> On a voyage unto a port beyond the sea,
> And I watched a gallant soldier, as he bade his last farewell
> To the lassie he loved most tenderly.
> And I heard the soldier promise to the lassie now in tears:
> "When the fields are white with daisies I'll return".

The soldier is inevitably killed and as the 'lass' is weeping, she hears a voice beside her whisper,

> ... 'My dear':
> God has spared me for your keeping, and the promise once I made,
> When the fields are white with daisies I'll return.

George Beavis died of wounds in a Casualty Clearing Station in Dickebusch. According to a letter from the Officer in Charge of the 1st Field Ambulance, written on 1 February 1918 to the Australian Red Cross Society Wounded and Missing Enquiry Bureau:

> ... he was admitted to the Dressing Station of this Ambulance on the night of 20.9.17 with shell wound of right leg, the wounds being so extensive as to necessitate amputation of the leg. He was suffering a good deal from shock, and died next morning. The burial took place at Military Huts Cemetery Dickebusch.

In memory Of the dearly loved son Of J.H. Phillips of Brisbane

PRIVATE ROBERT SIDNEY PHILLIPS
AUSTRALIAN INFANTRY
DIED 23 SEPTEMBER 1917 AGED 23
BURIED YPRES RESERVOIR CEMETERY

When 'Sid' Phillips' father asked the Australian Red Cross Wounded and Missing Enquiry Bureau for information about his son's death, it would be interesting to know what he was told. The witnesses all agreed that he was dead but their accounts differed materially:

Sgt Ward, interviewed 25.1.18

> He was badly wounded in the legs and body during the hop over at Ypres. I saw him immediately after he was hit, his right leg was practically off. He later drew his revolver and blew his brains out. I did not see this happen. I don't know where he was buried.

Sgt Thomas interviewed 3.4.18

> I saw him after he was killed on September 25th at Passchendaele; he had been blown out of a shell hole and twisted like a corkscrew. He crawled back into a shell hole and blew his head off with a rifle.

Pte Kenny interviewed 2.5.18

> Phillips was coming out without his gas helmet and was in the main street of Ypres when a red cap turned him back – he had not gone more than a few yards when he was hit by a shell and only lived about half an hour. They carried him to a Dressing Station which was near the Cloth Hall in the town. I did not see this but I saw our chaps going up to bury him – I believe he was buried near the Dressing Station.

Three witnesses in the file say that Phillips shot himself, but the fact that he is buried in Ypres Reservoir Cemetery would indicate that it was Private Kenny who was talking about the right man. His father would have preferred this; Phillips was a Roman Catholic and to a Roman Catholic suicide is a mortal sin.

KILLED IN ACTION JESU MERCY

THE REVEREND BENJAMIN CORRIE RUCK-KEENE
ARMY CHAPLAINS' DEPARTMENT
DIED 26 SEPTEMBER 1917 AGED 28
BURIED YPRES RESERVOIR CEMETERY

It is not unusual to see 'Killed in action' on a headstone but it is unusual if it's on the grave of an army padre. Padres were not armed men; they did not take part in attacks but this didn't mean they were never seen in the front line. Initially they had been forbidden from going any further forward than the advanced dressing stations. But many went up into the trenches knowing that the soldiers appreciated their presence, and knowing that they could make themselves useful: helping with the wounded, staying with the dying, talking to the men. One of the most famous of all wartime chaplains, the Revd Geoffrey Studdart Kennedy, had this advice to give:

> Live with the men, go everywhere they go. Make up your mind you will share all their risks, and more, if you can do any good. The line is the key to the whole business. Work in the very front and they will listen to you; but if you stay behind, you're wasting your time. Men will forgive you anything but lack of courage and devotion.

According to *The Times*, Ruck-Keene was killed 'by a shell in the regimental aid post'; further forward than the advanced dressing stations, regimental aid posts were usually just metres from the front line trenches.

The son of the vicar of St Michael and All Angels, Copford, Essex, Ruck-Keene had been a curate at St James the Great in Bethnal Green. His mother chose his inscription. She used the phrase 'Jesu mercy', a shorthand prayer for the deceased to be spared the pains of hell, which would suggest that the family were High Church Anglicans since she used it for her other son too, Captain Ralph Ruck-Keene, who was killed in January 1916:

> Killed in a bombing accident
> On active service
> Jesu mercy

By the Path of Duty R.I.P.

PRIVATE ROBERT SAMUEL WADE
LINCOLNSHIRE REGIMENT
DIED 26 SEPTEMBER 1917 AGED 22
BURIED BRIDGE HOUSE CEMETERY

Private Wade's inscription quotes a phrase from the commemorative scroll sent to the next-of-kin of all the dead once the war was over. Underneath the royal crest, the scroll recorded the deceased's rank, name and regiment with the following wording:

> He [or She] whom this scroll commemorates was numbered among those who, at the call of King and Country, left all that was dear to them, endured hardness, faced danger, and finally passed out of the sight of men by the path of duty and self sacrifice, giving up their own lives that others might live in freedom. Let those who come after see to it that his name be not forgotten.

The medieval scholar and ghost story writer MR James composed the words, changing them at King George V's request from 'at the bidding of their country', to 'at the call of King and Country'. James appears to have captured the mood of the time and his words were much quoted on war memorials and in headstone inscriptions, especially the last line – 'Let those who come after see to it that his / their / her name be not forgotten'.

The Wades were a military family. Robert's father, James Wade, had served in the South African War where he had been wounded and taken prisoner. Having retired, he re-enlisted in the reserve in September 1914. Robert's eldest brother, William, was a regular soldier, he died of wounds on 25 October 1914, and their uncle, Samuel, their father's brother, also a regular soldier, was killed in action six weeks later on 8 December. Robert Wade was killed at Polygon Wood and buried at Bridge House Cemetery where all but one of the 45 burials relate to either the 25th or 26th September 1917.

THE LOVE THAT LINGERS O'ER HIS NAME IS MORE THAN FAME

SERJEANT GEORGE HARRY BRAMMAGE
LEICESTERSHIRE REGIMENT
DIED 28 SEPTEMBER 1917 AGED 23
BURIED DOCHY FARM NEW BRITISH CEMETERY

From all the indications, George Brammage was a fairly exceptional young man. His medal roll index card shows that he was not entitled to the 1914-15 Star, which means that he didn't serve in a theatre of war until after 1915, yet by September 1917 he was a serjeant. His pre-war trade had been shoemaking and in the 1911 census, when he was 15, he gave his trade as a shoe clicker. This was one of the best-paid jobs in the industry since shoe clicking, cutting the uppers from the leather skins, was highly skilled.

His mother signed for his inscription. The lines come from the third verse of Oliver Wendell Holmes' poem, *In Memory of John and Robert Ware*:

> A whiter soul, a fairer mind,
> A life with purer course and aim,
> A gentler eye, a voice more kind,
> We may not look on earth to find.
> The love that lingers o'er his name
> Is more than fame.

John Ware was an American surgeon who died in 1864, the same year that his son, Robert, also a surgeon, serving with the 44th Massachusetts Infantry, was killed in action during the American Civil War.

Brammage served with the 2nd/5th Battalion Leicestershire Regiment, which spent eight months of 1916 in Ireland – explaining why Brammage was so late entering a threatre of war. In January 1917 the battalion was sent to France. After a few months on the Somme it moved to Ypres. Brammage was killed in the trenches at Hill 37 near Polygon Wood.

STRAIGHT OF LIMB TRUE OF EYE STEADY AND AGLOW

SECOND LIEUTENANT GEORGE FREDERICK WHITBY HARRISON
WILTSHIRE REGIMENT
DIED 30 SEPTEMBER 1917 AGED 23
BURIED KEMMEL CHATEAU MILITARY CEMETERY

They went with songs to the battle, they were young,
Straight of limb, true of eye, steady and aglow.
They were staunch to the end against odds uncounted,
They fell with their faces to the foe.

For all its terrible splendour, few people will probably be able to identify the poem from which this inscription comes. It's the next verse by which it is known:

They shall grow not old, as we that are left grow old:
Age shall not weary them, nor the years condemn.
At the going down of the sun and in the morning
We will remember them.

Laurence Binyon's *For the Fallen* was published on 21 September 1914, just two months after the outbreak of war. It immediately became popular and has remained popular ever since having become an integral part of our Remembrance Day services.

Before the war, George Harrison, the eldest child of Ernest Harrison a commercial traveller in cigars, was a cutter in the clothing trade. The family lived in Leicester. He served with the 3rd Battalion Wiltshire Regiment but at the time of his death was one of fourteen officers who had just been attached to the 6th. He was killed four nights later whilst supervising a working party.

He gave his life for another

CAPTAIN WILFRID THOMAS CHANING-PEARCE MC
ROYAL ARMY MEDICAL CORPS
DIED 1 OCTOBER 1917 AGED 32
BURIED DERRY HOUSE CEMETERY NO. 2

Wilfrid Chaning-Pearce's sister, Eleanor, chose his inscription, underestimating by hundreds the number of men who owed their lives to him. Educated at Rugby, Emmanuel College Cambridge and Guy's Hospital, Chaning-Peace was a newly qualified doctor when the war broke out. He joined up immediately. Attached to the King's Liverpool Regiment, he served at the front through the battles of the Somme, Arras and Messines Ridge, admired, as his Colonel told the family, for 'his absolute contempt for danger and cheerful endurance of exposure and hardship'.

Another colleague told them that everyone was extremely glad when he was awarded a Military Cross for his actions on 31 July 1917 when:

> he moved his aid post forward at a very early period of the fight, quite regardless of any danger to himself, but only thinking how he could give the quickest help and be of the greatest service to the wounded.

He worked for 36 hours without a break and then fell into such a deep sleep that when he woke it was to find himself being carried away in an ambulance.

It was this disregard for danger that was the cause of his death. He went out into No Man's Land in broad daylight to locate some wounded men and was shot at close range by a German sentry. That night, the men recovered his body at their second attempt; he was buried the following day.

"THE WORLD SHALL END WHEN I FORGET" SWINBURNE

SECOND LIEUTENANT DOUGLAS TOWRY FARRIER
ROYAL GARRISON ARTILLERY
DIED 1 OCTOBER 1917 AGED 29
BURIED VOORMEZEELE ENCLOSURES NO. 1 AND NO. 2

Mrs Netta Farrier chose her husband's inscription from Swinburne's *Itylus*, based on the Greek legend of Aedon who is stricken with grief and remorse having accidentally killed her daughter, Itylus. The gods take pity on her and turn her into a nightingale. In Swinburne's poem, a nightingale sorrowfully contrasts a swallow's carefree existence, its ability to carry on its life as if nothing has happened, with its own unending heartbreak. Many of the bereaved must have felt the same – how could the world carry on as though nothing had happened. John Oxenham (William Arthur Dunckerley 1852-1941) touched on it in his poem, *To You Who Have Lost* (1915):

> I know! I know!
> The ceaseless ache, the emptiness, the woe, –
> The pang of loss, –
> The strength that sinks beneath so sore a cross,
> " – Heedless and careless, still the world wags on,
> And leaves me broken ... Oh, my son! my son!"

Oxenham's comfort was to tell relations:

> He died the noblest death a man may die,
> Fighting for God and Right and Liberty; -
> And such a death is immortality.

Swinburne's nightingale received no comfort.

Given by a loving father and mother with proud but aching hearts

GUNNER FRANCIS JOSEPH GELL
AUSTRALIAN HEAVY ARTILLERY
DIED 4 OCTOBER 1917 AGED 23
BURIED YPRES RESERVOIR CEMETERY.

Who else 'gave' their son? It was God:

> For God so loved the world, that he gave his only begotten Son, that whosoever believeth in him should not perish, but have everlasting life.
>
> John 3:16

Without any intended blasphemy, many parents like the Gells believed that, in the same way that God had sacrificed His son for the sake of mankind, so too had they sacrificed theirs. It was an idea confirmed in Sir John Arkwright's wonderful old Remembrance Day hymn, *O Valiant Hearts*:

> These were His servants, in His steps they trod,
> Following through death the martyred Son of God:
> Victor, He Rose; victorious too shall rise
> They who have drunk His cup of sacrifice.

Francis Gell, a sign writer and printer from Geelong in Victoria, enlisted in December 1915. He served with the 55th Battery, 36th Australian Heavy Artillery Brigade, which had just taken delivery of its brand-new 9.2-inch howitzers. These were the seriously big guns. With a working crew of fourteen, they could fire their 132 kg shells almost 10 kilometres. Normally kept well behind the lines, the guns were occasionally moved forward at which point they became extremely vulnerable should the German guns get their range. This is what happened the day Gell was killed, the opening day of the Battle of Broodseinde.

Gell's mother appealed to the Australian Red Cross Wounded and Missing Enquiry Bureau for information. All the witnesses were agreed that the gun had received a direct hit; some were specific about the casualties – fourteen killed and seventeen wounded. The witnesses were again united about Gell's fate, but less so about the details: 'I saw him afterwards; he was just recognisable'; 'There were several bodies unrecognisable, and Gell was amongst them'.

It is men of my age and single who are expected to do their duty

PRIVATE WILLIAM HENRY RICKARD
AUSTRALIAN INFANTRY
DIED 4 OCTOBER 1917 AGED 25
BURIED LIJSSENTHOEK MILITARY CEMETERY

As the casualties mounted so the demand for recruits intensified and the numbers of those prepared to enlist dropped. Recruiting posters exhorted Australian men to join up and defend the Empire, warning them that if England fell Australia would fall too and that the Germans would treat Australian women worse than they had the Belgians. Many people thought the Government should introduce conscription – and many people disagreed. This eventually led to two referendums on the question, both of which the Government lost.

A fire-brick maker, who described his other skills as engine driving and mechanical drawing, Rickard enlisted in April 1916. You can see the way his mind was working from the inscription his father chose – he felt he should do his duty. He left Australia with the 16th reinforcements on 13 October 1916, just two weeks before the first referendum, which resulted in a defeat for the Government – 1,087, 557 votes in favour and 1,160,033 against.

Arriving in France in December 1916, Rickard served with the 28th Battalion Australian Infantry. He was wounded in the thigh in March 1917, spent five months in hospital in England before returning to the front in August. On 4 October the battalion took part in the attack on Broodseinde Ridge. Rickard was again wounded and died the same day in a Casualty Clearing Station at Lijssenthoek of 'shrapnel wounds on the head'. The battalion war diary described how by 12 noon:

> Repeated counter attacks failed under our effective artillery fire. Throughout the period enemy heavily shelled our newly gained position ... Casualties: Officers wounded 6, O/RKS K 42, W 85, M 5

When alive they would not take your place they cannot have it now my son

PRIVATE WALTER JOHN SAYERS
AUSTRALIAN INFANTRY
DIED 4 OCTOBER 1917 AGED 34
BURIED AEROPLANE CEMETERY

This is another inscription that references the controversy in Australia over the question of conscription. Australia needed to provide reinforcements at the rate of 5,500 men a month in order to maintain its overseas forces at an operational level. The first referendum on the issue having been defeated in October 1916, the Government held a second one in December 1917 as Australia was now being asked to raise 7,000 men a month. This time it was defeated 1,015,159 in favour and 1,181,747 against. The question went away but the passions raised had been deeply divisive both socially and politically.

Walter John Sayers, a farmer from Wycheproof, a small community in north-western Victoria, enlisted on 17 August 1916 aged 33, responding to the call for more volunteers having not enlisted earlier. He trained as a Lewis gunner, served with the 7th Infantry Battalion, and was killed in the attack on Broodseinde Ridge.

The 7th Infantry Battalion's digitised war diary provides every detail of the attack; the following paragraph comes from the narrative of operations:

> At 0530 enemy put down on the Bn. assembly position a heavy barrage of all calibres causing many casualties. It was impossible to move the Bn. to avoid the barrage. The Bn. endured the terrific barrage with great steadiness and courage and when our barrage opened at 0600 the Bn. rose and quietly moved forward through the enemy barrage to the attack.

Private Sayer's widowed mother chose his inscription. Addressed to her son, it rebukes those who wouldn't volunteer, 'would not take your place' and defiantly asserts that they can't have it now, referring to the place he has won for himself by his sacrifice in heaven.

One of God's good men

PRIVATE ARTHUR BRIDGE
EAST LANCASHIRE REGIMENT
DIED 4 OCTOBER 1917 AGED 30
BURIED CEMENT HOUSE CEMETERY

God's Good Man is the title of a novel by the best-selling Edwardian novellist, Marie Corelli. It's a love story between the eponymous hero, the Reverend John Walden, and the wealthy, spoilt Maryllia Vancourt – who is reformed by the love of a good man. Published in 1904, the book was made into a film in 1919.
And what were the qualities of one of God's good men?

> ... he was physically sound and morally healthy, and lived, as it were, on the straight line from earth to heaven, beginning each day as if it were his first life-opportunity, and ending it soberly with prayer, as though it were his last.

On 1 December 1917, the *Burnley Express* reported that Mrs Bridges,

> ... would be grateful to any soldier who could give her any tidings concerning the fate of her husband, Signaller Arthur Bridge 242113, East Lancashire Regiment. She has officially been notified that he is wounded and missing after an engagement on November 4th.

Seven months later the newspaper carried another report: Bridges had gone missing on 4 October, not 4 November, and had been left in the care of three RAMC men but, as nothing had since been heard of him, he was now presumed to have died on that day.

"I'M ALL RIGHT MOTHER CHEERIO"

LIEUTENANT HAROLD ROWLAND HILL
AUSTRALIAN INFANTRY
DIED 4 OCTOBER 1917 AGED 22
BURIED BUTTES NEW BRITISH CEMETERY

What would you say to your mother as you signed off your letter to her just before you went up into the front line? You'd tell her that you were OK. And since the inscription, chosen by Lieutenant Hill's mother, is in quotation marks surely the words are his, probably the last words he wrote to her.

Hill served with the 25th Battalion Australian Infantry. On the night of the 1/2 October the Battalion arrived at Esplanade Saps, Zonnebeke with an effective strength of 35 officers and 989 other ranks. The 3rd was spent, 'In Front Line', on the night of the 3rd/4th the War Dairy recorded:

> Jumping off tape was laid by midnight along frontage and along Coy. flanks. The Battalion was on same by 4.30am on 4th. At zero the Bn. closed up to within 50 yards of barrage and fought its way to the objective where it consolidated.

The battalion moved back into the support lines on 7 October by which time two officers and 38 other ranks had been killed, 10 officers and 185 other ranks wounded and 16 other ranks were missing – a total of 25% of the battalion.

Witnesses for the Australian Red Cross Wounded and Missing Enquiry Bureau state that:

> Lieutenant Hill was killed before the hopover just behind Zonnebeke, near Zonnebeke Church. He was with Brigade Sig. at the time in charge of 25th Hd. Qrts. Sig.
>
> He led the 7th Bde. Signallers advance party over the top, near Zonnebeke about 6.30 am on Oct. 4/17. I was quite close to him when he was severely wounded during the heavy barrage, and was taken by S/Bs to the Menin Road Hospital near the Comforts Fund.
>
> I helped to bandage Lt. Hill. He was so badly wounded in the head and hit almost all over his body too, that he could not have lived more than an hour if that. Afterwards I heard that he had lived nearly two hours.

TO THEM THAT SAVED OUR HERITAGE AND CAST THEIR OWN AWAY

CAPTAIN ROBERT SEFTON ADAMS
ROYAL FIELD ARTILLERY
DIED 5 OCTOBER 1917 AGED 29
BURIED ZANTVOORDE BRITISH CEMETERY

In May 1922 King George V made a visit to the battlefield cemeteries of the Western Front. He wanted no fanfare; he was coming to pay his respects to the dead. A few days later, *The Times* published a poem by Rudyard Kipling called *The King's Pilgrimage*. Captain Adam's wife quoted from the final verse for her husband's inscription:

Our King went forth on pilgrimage
His prayers and vows to pay
To them that saved our heritage
And cast their own away.

Robert Sefton Adams was brought up in New Zealand, but had he served with a New Zealand regiment he would not have had an inscription since the New Zealand Government objected to the War Graves Commission's charge of 3½d a letter, believing it to be against their principle of equality.

Adams, having come to England to study law, was married and living in Southsea, Hampshire when war broke out. He joined up, served with the 12th Battery, 35th Brigade, Royal Field Artillery and was killed in action on 5 October 1917. His wife in England chose his inscription but his original, temporary wooden grave marker is kept in St Mary's Anglican Church, Silverstream, New Zealand, where his parents lived.

The last verse of Kipling's poem raises an interesting question: what would the dead think of today's popular view that the war was a futile waste.

All that they had they gave – they gave –
In sure and single faith.
There can no knowledge reach the grave
To make them grudge their death
Save only if they understood
That, after all was done,
We they redeemed denied their blood
And mocked the gains it won.

Rock of Ages Cleft for Me

PRIVATE JOSEPH PERCY COOPER
AUSTRALIAN INFANTRY
DIED 5 OCTOBER 1917 AGED 19
BURIED SANCTUARY WOOD CEMETERY

This is among the most popular of all the hymns quoted in inscriptions, a favourite nineteenth century hymn appearing in virtually every Protestant hymnal – of which there were fifty-two.

> Rock of ages cleft for me,
> Let me hide myself in Thee;
> Let the water and the blood,
> From Thy riven side which flowed,
> Be of sin the double cure,
> Cleanse me from its guilt and power.

Christ is the Rock of Ages from whose side water and blood flowed at his crucifixion. Private Cooper was initially listed as missing. His parents instituted a Red Cross search from which it was possible to piece together what happened:

> Informant states that the 26th A.I.F. were going into the line at Zonnebeke at about 8 pm on Oct/4th/17 when Cooper was struck by a shell and killed instantly, a piece of shell went right through his lungs. Private V.H. Lusk

> I saw him killed on the tape just as we left the duck boards to go over at Zonnebeke on the 4th October about 4.30 am. A whizz-bang killed him and Whipler and wounded several. Private J.S. Locke

> I buried my comrade 400 yards from Zonnebeke Church as near as possible. ... The said soldier was a dear friend of mine and ... I would like his parents to know his comrades buried him decently. Private G. Graham

"TIS SWEET TO DIE FOR ONE'S COUNTRY"

SERGEANT STUART NORMAN SPENCE
AUSTRALIAN INFANTRY
DIED 7 OCTOBER 1917 AGED 41
BURIED LIJSSENTHOEK MILITARY CEMETERY

This is a partial translation of Horace's famous line: 'Dulce et decorum est pro patria mori'. It may seem incredible that after the savaging Wilfred Owen gave this line anyone would want to use it for their son's headstone inscription. But at this period, Horace was still more powerful than Owen. Owen contrasts the reality of death in battle with the 'old lie' that 'It is sweet and meet to die for one's country'. The translation is Owen's; others translate 'decorum' as glorious.

> ...
> If in some smothering dreams you too could pace
> Behind the wagon that we flung him in,
> And watch the white eyes writhing in his face,
> His hanging face, like a devil's sick of sin;
> If you could hear, at every jolt, the blood
> Come gargling from his froth-corrupted lungs,
> Obscene as cancer, bitter as the cud
> Of vile, incurable sores on innocent tongues,
> My friend, you would not tell with such high zest
> To children ardent for some desperate glory,
> The old Lie; Dulce et Decorum est
> Pro patria mori.

Owen denied that there was anything sweet, meet or glorious about the process of dying for your country. Horace's assertion was that to die for your country won you glory.

Norman Spence emigrated to Australia when he was 32. Nine years later he enlisted and returned to Britain. He served with the 41st Battalion Australian Infantry, which took part in the attack on Broodseinde Ridge on 4 October. Spence survived the attack but the next day was wounded in the right shoulder and hip by a shell. He died two days later.

ONE WHO LOVED HIS FELLOW MEN

CAPTAIN REGINALD SHERMAN
ROYAL ARMY MEDICAL CORPS
DIED 10 OCTOBER 1917 AGED 30
BURIED CANADA FARM CEMETERY

To love your fellow man is evidence of your love for God, this was the conclusion of the poet Leigh Hunt (1784-1859) in his poem *Abou Ben Adhem*. One night an angel appeared to Ben Adhem; it was writing in a book. Ben Adhem asked the angel what it was writing and the angel replied, 'the names of those who love the Lord'. Ben Adhem asked if his name was among them and the angel replied, 'No'. Not unduly concerned, Ben Adhem said, 'cheerily', 'I pray thee, then, write me as one that loves his fellow men'. The next day the angel appeared again:

> And showed the names whom love of God had blest,
> And lo! Ben Adhem's name led all the rest.

This was Leigh Hunt's best-known work, and the words, 'One that loved his fellow men' were not only carved on his own headstone in Kensal Green Cemetery but became a popular tribute to men who were judged to have done good in their lives, as Captain Sherman had done.

Sherman was a doctor. Trained at St Batholomew's, he joined the RAMC in December 1914, went to France in February 1915 and served with the 4th Field Ambulance throughout 1915 and 1916. On 10 October 1917:

> He was shot in the chest while visiting the forward aid-posts and died peacefully in the dressing station some hours later. *The Times* 23 October 1917

A fellow officer and friend told his family:

> Everyone is quite heart-broken and everywhere you hear nothing but words of regret at his death. He was always the centre of any fun or frolic and always ready to take a large share of any hardships that were going. He was a large-hearted, generous man, and as brave as a lion.

The Lord watch between me and thee when we are absent one from another

LIEUTENANT COLONEL ARCHIBALD JOHN SALTREN-WILLETT
ROYAL GARRISON ARTILLERY
DIED 11 OCTOBER 1917 AGED 51
BURIED VLAMERTINGHE NEW MILITARY CEMETERY

> *Western Morning News* Saturday 20 October 1917
> Lt-Col Archibald John Saltren-Willett (killed in action on Oct.11) was the son of the late Capt. John Saltren-Willett, of Petticombe, Torrington, and Newington House, Oxford. He was born in 1866, and after leaving Cheltenham, entered the RMA; he passed out of Woolwich into the Royal Artillery in April 1885, reaching the rank of lieut-col. in Feb. 1913. He had served on the Staff as Assistant Inspector of Warlike Stores.

This prosaic death announcement contrasts markedly with the routine order circulated round the 1st ANZAC Corps Heavy Artillery two days after Saltren-Willett's death:

> SECRET: Routine Order No: 62 13th October 1917
> Obituary: It is with deep regret that the B.G.H.A. announces that Lieut-Colonel A.J. Saltren-Willett, Commanding 66th H.A.G. was killed in action on the 11th instant. Full of energy, and at all times keenly solicitous for the welfare of those serving under him, the loss of this gallant officer will be deeply felt by those serving under him so recently, and by the Royal Regiment in general.

So, far from being in charge of 'warlike stores', Saltren-Willett was commanding a 1st ANZAC Heavy Artillery Battery Group, had been on active service since October 1916 and was Mentioned in Despatches for his untiring supervision of his group of counter-batteries during the offensive East of Ypres in June, July, August and September 1917. He was killed instantaneously the following month by a fragment of shell whilst directing his batteries. His wife chose his lovely inscription, the wife who doesn't get a mention in any of the newspaper announcements. It comes from Genesis 31:49 and has come to be used as a farewell blessing often represented by the single word Mizpah.

He loved honour More than he feared death

LIEUTENANT DAVID GUNN
SEAFORTH HIGHLANDERS
DIED 13 OCTOBER 1917 AGED 22
BURIED PASSCHENDAELE NEW BRITISH CEMETERY

David Gunn's father, John, chose his inscription, quite possibly influenced by a popular print of the time by the American artist and illustrator Howard Chandler Christy, which was called, *The Field of Honour*. Underneath the image of an angel crowning a dead Belgian soldier with a laurel wreath are the words, 'He loved honour more than he feared death'. Quoted from Shakespeare's *Julius Caesar*, these are the words Brutus used to tell Cassius that he would prefer to die rather than to lose his honourable reputation:

> Set honour in one eye and death i' th' other,
> And I will look upon both indifferently,
> For let the gods so speed me as I love
> The name of honour more than I fear death.

In 1911, aged 15, David Gunn was a stockbrokers' clerk living at home with his parents in South Norwood. He volunteered soon after the outbreak of war and served as a private in the Cameron Highlanders, arriving in France on 19 February 1915. Commissioned into the Seaforth Highlanders, Gunn was killed in action on the second day of the First Battle of Passchendaele. His body was found in an unmarked grave three years later in May 1920, still with its identity discs.

A HAPPY WARRIOR

PRIVATE HARRY NOEL LEA
AUSTRALIAN INFANTRY
DIED 14 OCTOBER 1917 AGED 21
BURIED YPRES RESERVOIR CEMETERY

'Who is the happy warrior? Who is he, that every man in arms would wish to be?' So asked Wordsworth in his 1807 poem *The Happy Warrior*. He then gave the answer: a man who is brave, modest, faithful, resolute, diligent and magnanimous, an honourable man, a man of high endeavour guided by reason and duty, a home loving man and thus 'more brave for this, that he hath much to love' – and much to lose.

The term gained in stature throughout the nineteenth century, enhanced by G.F. Watts' painting of 'The Happy Warrior', which showed a young knight on the point of death being embraced by an ethereal figure. By the beginning of the twentieth century the phrase had become a universal term of approval for someone who had led a good life serving the state.

Harry Noel Lea, a bank clerk from Sydney, enlisted on 15 January 1917, served with the 17th Australian Infantry, part of the 2nd Australian Division, and died of wounds received on 9 October when the Division was in action at Poelcapelle. Although his mother instituted a Red Cross search no one could tell exactly what had happened to him but one of his friends wrote to say that, 'I wandered around Ypres for some time visiting the various cemeteries and at last came across my pal's grave in the 'Prison' cemetery right in the heart of Ypres'.

I COULD NOT LOVE YOU DEAR SO WELL LOVED I NOT HONOR MORE

SERGEANT HAROLD FULLER PARSONS
AUSTRALIAN INFANTRY
DIED 15 OCTOBER 1917 AGED 36
BURIED TYNE COT CEMETERY

> Harold Parsons was a Cpl. and temporary Sgt. in S.Coy.V. ... He was neither dark nor fair, slight moustache, about 5 ft. 8. and about 30 and married. He had some children but I don't know how many. I was with Parsons in a trench ... near Zonnebeke ... I had just moved away from him for a moment when some shrapnel burst over us and I saw Parsons hit in the throat and killed immediately ... We lifted Parsons from the trench on to the parapet and covered him up with his ground sheet. He was buried at dusk just behind our trench.
>
> Pte G.Todd 2896 to the Red Cross Australian Wounded and Missing Enquiry Bureau

As another witness told the Red Cross, "It was just a casual shell".
Mrs Elizabeth Parson's chose her husband's inscription, based on the last two lines of *To Lucasta Going to the Wars* by the Cavalier poet, Richard Lovelace (1617-1657). There was no conscription in Australia, Parsons, a thirty-six-year-old married man was under no compulsion to go and fight.

> Tell me not, sweet, I am unkind,
> That from the nunnery
> Of that chaste breast and quiet mind
> To war and arms I fly.
> True, a new mistress now I chase,
> The first foe in the field;
> And with a stronger faith embrace
> A sword, a horse, a shield.
> Yet this inconstancy is such
> As thou too shalt adore;
> I could not love thee, Dear, so much,
> Loved I not honour more.

A SOLDIER AND A MAN

LANCE CORPORAL WILLIAM GAYNER SMITH
SOUTH AFRICAN INFANTRY
DIED 15 OCTOBER 1917 AGED 34
BURIED BUFFS ROAD CEMETERY

> On the night of the 13th the 2nd and 4th South African Regiments moved up to the front line, taking over trenches held by part of the 26th and 27th Brigades, which had been engaged in that attack on the 12th which was foiled by the disastrous weather. The relief was very difficult for the whole country had become an irreclaimable bog, and the mud was beyond all human description. There was intermittent shelling during the 14th and 15th, and much bombing from enemy planes.
>
> *History of the South African Forces in the Great War* John Buchan

Born in Bristol, Smith emigrated to South Africa and joined the police, immediately enlisting in the South African Infantry on the outbreak of war. In October 1916, he got married in Bristol, the *Bristol Mercury* reporting that, 'owing to the bridegroom having only recently recovered from wounds received in action in July last in France the wedding was of a quiet nature'. Killed twelve months later, Smith's wife chose his inscription. There are several possible sources but the two strongest are both music hall songs. In one a soldier surveys the battlefield and laments how far he is from everyone he loves but acknowledges that: 'I am, whate'er else my fate a soldier and a man'. A concept reinforced by the refrain: 'Remember him who yields his life is a soldier and a man'. The other song was probably better known. Written and composed in 1900 by Joseph Tabrar (1875-1931), the song builds up an image of a girl's best man, each verse emphasising another quality that makes him 'a soldier and a man':

> Though he's a soldier, a common soldier
> He has got the pluck and muscle for a soldier
> And I'm proud to say the dear's
> One of the Dublin Fusiliers
> And he's proved himself a soldier and a man.

Lance Corporal William Smith's headstone in Buff's Road Cemetery

HE GAVE HIS LIFE FOR HIS COMRADES

SERJEANT JAMES BREMNER
ROYAL GARRISON ARTILLERY
DIED 15 OCTOBER 1917 AGED 32
BURIED BUS HOUSE CEMETERY

> Greater love hath no man than this, that a man lay down his life for his friends.

The words of St John Chapter XV verse 13 form one of the most popular of all headstone inscriptions and war memorial dedications. But Serjeant Bremner's sister, in paraphrasing St John, chose the word comrade rather than friend, her brother gave his life for his comrades, his brothers-in-arms.

The sense of comradeship, a feeling of fellowship with those in your regiment, company, platoon or section, was one of the defining qualities of the First World War. In his memoir, *With a Machine Gun to Cambrai*, George Coppard wrote:

> Of my memories of life in the trenches, the one thing I cherish more than anything else is the comradeship that grew up between us as a result of the way of life we were compelled to lead – living together under the open sky, night and day, fair weather or foul, witnessing death or injury, helping in matters of urgency, and above all, facing the enemy. Such situations were the solid foundation on which our comradeship was built. It has been said that such comradeship died when the war ended.

It has not been possible to tell whether Bremner's sister, Ina, was referring to a specific incident in her brother's inscription, or just speaking generally about her brother's motivation. Bremner was the only member of the 251st Siege Battery to die on that day.

In the words of his colonel He was an example to all

SECOND LIEUTENANT DOUGLAS FITCH
ROYAL FIELD ARTILLERY
DIED 16 OCTOBER 1917 AGED 20
BURIED LA CLYTTE MILITARY CEMETERY

> In loving memory of
> Douglas Fitch
> Second Lieutenant Royal Field Artillery
> Born 25th October 1896, fell in action near
> Ypres 16th October 1917
> A most gallant officer, beloved of his men. Throughout the hard and dangerous work of the last few weeks of his life he never spared himself and he was an example to us all.
>
> Memorial plaque St Andrew's Church, Kingswood, Surrey

Charles Fitch quoted from the letter of condolence he'd received from his son's colonel both on his headstone inscription and on his brass memorial plaque in St Andrew's Church. There's more information about Fitch in the Marquis de Ruvigny's *Roll of Honour*, where Fitch's Battery Commander and his captain are quoted as saying:

> Always thoughtful for others, whether they were his brother officers or the men of his section; always cheerful, he had a wonderful effect on us all and I think it was a good deal due to his influence that the battery has faced a very hard gruelling without a murmuring.
>
> His unfailing cheerfulness and unconcern through the heaviest shell fire and greatest discomforts were wonderful ... There was no more popular officer in the brigade and the men of his battery and especially those of his own section, almost worshipped him.

Douglas Fitch, who served with 'C' Battery 162nd Brigade, was killed in action just ten days before his twenty-first birthday. He was his parents' only child.

HE LEFT HIS HOME TO GIVE HIS ALL FOR THE SAKE OF CIVILIZATION

PRIVATE CHARLES EDWIN HABGOOD
ROYAL FUSILIERS
DIED 17 OCTOBER 1917 AGED 35
BURIED DOZINGHEM MILITARY CEMETERY

Where did Mrs Sarah Habgood, Private Habgood's wife, get the idea that her husband had given 'his all for the sake of civilization'? The answer is probably from the back of the Victory Medal that he, as a member of the Allied armed services, would automatically have received having served in a theatre of war between 5 August 1914 and 11 November 1918. Soldiers continued to be eligible for the medal post-Armistice if they served in Transcapia (Turkmenistan) and Northern Russia in 1919. On the front of the medal there's a robed, winged figure – a winged victory – and on the reverse a laurel wreath with the words, 'The Great War for Civilisation'. (Mrs Habgood spelt it with a 'z', the medal with an 's').

Throughout the war British propaganda demonised the Germans, describing them as barbarians, depicting them as apes in pickelhaubes, their hands covered in the blood of women and babies, their much vaunted claims to 'kultur' mocked with posters showing the burning of the medieval library at Louvain. This is why, when the war was over, the Victory Medal could claim that it had been 'The Great War for Civilisation'.

Charles Habgood served with the 36th Battalion Royal Fusiliers, a labour battalion formed in May 1916, which was originally used for unloading ships at Rouen. In April 1917 the battalion became the 106th Company Labour Corps. These Corps were often made up of men medically rated as below A1 fitness, sometimes as a result of wounds. However, this didn't mean that they were safe from the guns. Five men of the old 36th Battalion died in an unspecified incident near Boezinge on 14 October 1917, with sixteen dying of wounds from the same incident in the following days.

Dozinghem Military Cemetery

AGE 17 YRS. 1 MON. 10 DYS IN THY KEEPING OUR FATHER

GUNNER MAITLAND HAROLD GORING
CANADIAN FIELD ARTILLERY
DIED 19 OCTOBER 1917 AGED 17
BURIED BRANDHOEK NEW MILITARY CEMETERY NO. 3

> I, Maitland Harold Goring, do solemnly swear that the above are answers made by me to the above questions and that they are true ...
>
> Attestation Paper Canadian Over-seas Expeditionary Force

Maitland Harold Goring signed this form on 17 January 1917. One of the 'above' answers was to the question: what is your date of birth? To which young Maitland Goring had written, 9 September 1898. But this was a lie; Goring's date of birth was 9 September 1900. This explains why his mother was so specific about her son's age on his headstone. On the day he died, Goring was 17 years, one month and 10 days old. Soldiers were meant to be 18 before they could enlist and 19 before they went overseas. Did the fact that Goring named his grandmother as his next-of-kin have anything to do with this deception, the one his mother was determined to correct?

The Canadian Expeditionary Force burial register for Brandhoek Military Cemetery No. 3 recorded the circumstances of his death:

> 'Killed in action'
> He had just been dismissed from Parade, and was making for bivouac in Ypres area, when he was killed outright by a splinter from a bomb dropped from an enemy aeroplane.

Reader prepare to meet thy God

SAPPER ARTHUR OLIVER ELLIS
AUSTRALIAN ENGINEERS
DIED 21 OCTOBER 1917 AGED 32
BURIED TYNE COT CEMETERY

> Reader, prepare to meet thy God.
> Death is at no great distance; thou hast but a short time to do good. Acquire a heavenly disposition while here; for there will be no change after this life. ... In whatever disposition or state of soul thou diest, in that thou wilt be found in the eternal world. Death refines nothing, purifies nothing, kills no sin, helps to no glory. Let thy continual bent and inclination be to God, to holiness, to charity, to mercy, and to heaven: then, fall when thou mayest, thou wilt fall well.

Sapper Ellis's inscription, chosen by his stepmother, comes from the writings of the Methodist biblical scholar and theologian Adam Clarke (c1760-1832). It was not unusual to find the phrase on nineteenth-century gravestones. Since we know neither the day nor the hour when death will take us, we must live our lives in readiness; once we are dead it will be too late to change our ways and win our place in 'the eternal world'.

Sapper Ellis was a eucalyptus distiller from Macedon, Victoria, who enlisted in January 1916. Witnesses saw him killed on 21 October 1917, and some had identified his body, but after that the body was lost and not located until October 1920.

> I was told that a chap named Ellis was lying on the roadside killed. As I had a friend named Arthur Ellis I went up and found it was not my friend, but A.O.Ellis 7555. I saw his body, he had been killed by a shell up towards Westhoek Ridge, not far from Duckboard Walk. He had his disc on and I remember no. and initials.
>
> H.L.Harbison 7652 18 March 1918
> Witness to the Australian Red Cross Wounded and Missing Enquiry Bureau

A SOLDIER'S SON
GAVE HIS LIFE
FOR FREEDOM AND HONOUR
REST IN PEACE

LANCE CORPORAL ARCHIBALD NICHOLSON COE
SOUTH AFRICAN INFANTRY
DIED 21 OCTOBER 1917 AGED 24
BURIED CEMENT HOUSE CEMETERY

'He died for freedom and honour', these are the words on the bronze plaque distributed to the next-of-kin of everyone who died of whatever cause (except execution) whilst in the service of the Crown either at home or abroad between 4 August 1914 and 30 April 1919. The circular plaque, designed by Edward Carter Preston (1894-1965), features the figure of Britannia holding a laurel wreath over the casualty's name. Beside her is a lion, representing the British Empire and at the base of the plaque a much smaller lion savaging the Imperial German eagle. Manufacture began in December 1918 and eventually more than 1,000,000 were distributed, 600 of them to the next of kin of the women who died.

Many next-of-kin chose the exact words on the plaque for an inscription; Captain Richard James Coe modified them. His son '*gave* his life for freedom and honour', thus emphasising that he had been a volunteer not a conscript – not that there was any conscription in South Africa.

Lance Corporal Coe served with the 4th Regiment South African Infantry, known as the South African Scottish, which was part of the South African Brigade. The brigade arrived in Britain in November 1915, and in France in April 1916 where its legendary defence of Delville Wood in July 1916 resulted in huge casualties. 1917 saw the brigade take part in the battles of Arras and Third Ypres. On 13 October 1917 it moved into the front line trenches near Ypres. Although not involved in any action the four South African regiments were subject to heavy and continuous enemy shelling and aerial bombardment so that by the time they were relieved on 23 October the brigade had suffered 261 casualties killed and wounded. Coe was among the dead.

DEATH OPENS UNKNOWN DOORS
IT IS MOST GRAND TO DIE

LIEUTENANT DEREK EDWARD LEWIS VENN BAUMER
ROYAL FIELD ARTILLERY
DIED 21 OCTOBER 1917 AGED 20
BURIED SOLFERINO FARM CEMETERY

Baumer's inscription comes from John Masefield's play, *The Tragedy of Pompey the Great* (1910). The lines form part of a brief meditation on death over the body of Pompey's youthful commander, Valerius Flaccus. The 1st Centurion, looking at the body, remarks: 'Man is a sacred city, built of marvellous earth', to which the 2nd replies, 'Life was lived nobly here to give this body birth'. The 4th Centurian brings the conversation to the end a few lines later with the comment: 'Death opens unknown doors. It is most grand to die'. Impressed by the conversation, Ivor Gurney set it to music in a six-line song called *By a Bierside.* Gurney was serving in the front line at the time and wrote to tell a friend that, 'events yesterday gave one full opportunity to reflect on one's chances of doing that grand thing'. Baumer was the son of the *Punch* cartoonist and book illustrator, Lewis Baumer. Educated at Winchester College, he won a Classical Scholarship to New College, Oxford but on leaving school in 1914 instead of going up he joined up. He was still only 17 so it was January 1916, just after his nineteenth birthday, before he was sent to France. He served with the 86th Battery Royal Field Artillery and was killed near Langemarck when the battery came under fire. According to the Winchester College website, Baumer was 'running to the assistance of some of his men who had been buried by the burst of a shell' when he was wounded and died a few hours later. His commanding officer told his parents that this was typical behaviour of a man who had become 'one of my best subalterns and an officer of the very best type'. What made him of 'the very best type'? 'Under fire he was always cool'.

O THAT WE COULD HAVE CLASPED HIS HAND & SOOTHED HIS PARTING HOURS

SERGEANT GEORGE LOWBRIDGE
AUSTRALIAN INFANTRY
DIED 22 OCTOBER 1917 AGED 21
BURIED AEROPLANE CEMETERY

The nineteenth century idealised the 'good death': the loved one lying on their death bed, the family gathered round to say good-bye, hear their last words, hold their hand, comfort them. George Lowbridge's parents express the anguish so many families must have felt at not being able to do this. In addition, they couldn't attend the funeral, choose a headstone or visit the grave; in fact, all they could do was choose a personal inscription – if there was a body.

George Lowbridge was a bootmaker from Newcastle NSW. He enlisted in July 1915, left Australia that November and having spent some time in Egypt arrived in France in June 1916.

Travelling by train up from Marseilles he wrote to his parents:

> The air here is lovely and fresh, and all our boys are well. There is plenty of rain here; but we are glad of it after the heat and dryness of Egypt. It is like home here. It would do some of our Aus boys good to come here and learn a lesson – the slackers I mean. All that are left are the old men and women. Their sons have all gone to war.

In December 1916 Lowbridge was hospitalised in Britain with severe trench foot. He and a small party of men had been ordered to hold an advanced position, a crater, three-foot deep in water. The men's feet swelled so badly that they were forced to take their boots off. Expecting to be relieved after 48 hours they instead got the order to hold on for another 48. When relief did eventually arrive, the men had to be carried away on stretchers and it was touch and go whether Lowbridge's feet would have to be amputated or not.

He returned to the front in July 1917, was involved in the battles of the Menin Road, Polygon Wood and Broodeseinde then, just as the Australians were being withdrawn from the line to rest, he was killed by a shell whilst sheltering from a bombardment.

He set us always an example of cheerfulness and courage

MAJOR OWEN REGINALD SCHREIBER, MC AND BAR
ROYAL FIELD ARTILLERY
DIED 22 OCTOBER 1917 AGED 23
BURIED LIJSSENTHOEK MILITARY CEMETERY

Learn to be cheerful under difficulties, make little of the hardships you have to endure, never grumble, and do not forget that however bad things are they might be much worse.
A General's Letters to His Son on Obtaining His Commission

This little volume of twelve letters, published anonymously in 1917, gave advice on a whole range of subjects from discipline, 'the moral force which creates the essential difference between an army and a collection of men with muskets', to facing death, 'Should you ever be called on to perform a task which looks like spelling certain death, and honour and duty demand your doing it, you must, of course, not hesitate'.
Owen Schreiber, the son of Brigadier General AL Schreiber – who was not the author of the letters – certainly had the courage to perform a task that looked like spelling certain death. The citation for the bar to his Military Cross reads:

> For conspicuous gallantry in action. He extinguished a fire in a gun pit at great personal risk, removing 70 rounds of ammunition. During this period he was under intense shell fire.

Schreiber's inscription highlights the qualities soldiers of all ranks most admired in their fellow soldiers. Not, as those at home might assume, things like heroism, nobility or sacrifice, but courage, coolness and cheerfulness. These were all qualities that Schreiber, who crossed to France with the Expeditionary Force on 19 August 1914, must have possessed in full. Qualities that made him a major with an MC and Bar at the age of 23.

In the morn Those angel faces smile Long loved But only lost awhile

SERJEANT FRED IFOULD, MM
ROYAL FIELD ARTILLERY
DIED 23 OCTOBER 1917 AGED 26
BURIED BUFFS ROAD CEMETERY

Gunner Ifould, E Battery, Royal Field Artillery, was a member of the gun crew that on 22 August 1914 fired the first British artillery salvo of the war on the Western Front. However, whether Gunner Ifould was Fred or his brother Harry is not certain because they were both regular soldiers, both serving with E Battery at that time.

Which regiment and which gun fired this first shot has been the subject of some debate but the matter seems to have been settled on 22 August 1984 when, seventy years after the event, the descendants of E Battery, the 1st Regiment of Royal Horse Artillery, unveiled a plaque close by the spot. It is thought that this first salvo, fired in defence of the Scots Greys and 16th Lancers, was probably ineffective as the shells had been made in 1908.

Ifould's inscription is a contraction of some lines from verse three of Cardinal John Henry Newman's well-known hymn, *Lead Kindly Light Amid the Encircling Gloom*:

> So long Thy power hath blest me, sure it still
> Will lead me on.
> O'er moor and fen, o'er crag and torrent, till
> The night is gone,
> And with the morn those angel faces smile,
> Which I have loved long since, and lost awhile.

Harry Ifould survived the war, Fred Ifould, serving with D Battery, 155th Brigade, survived until October 1917 when he was killed in action near Ypres.

AND O' WE GRUDGED HIM SAIR TO THE LAND O' THE LEAL

PRIVATE KENNETH MOODIE MCBEAN
KING'S OWN SCOTTISH BORDERERS
DIED 25 OCTOBER 1917 AGED 19
BURIED DOZINGHEM MILITARY CEMETERY

Of Mrs Elizabeth McBean's three sons, Allan, serving with the Royal Scots, was killed in Gallipoli in June 1915, and Kenneth in Belgium in 1917. Allan has no grave and is commemorated on the Helles Memorial. Kenneth's inscription is therefore a lament for them both. It comes from *The Land of the Leal*, a poem by Caroline Oliphant, Lady Nairne (1766-1845) in which a mother describes how sorrow for her dead child is slowly killing her:

I'm wearin' awa', John
Like snaw-wreaths in thaw, John,
I'm wearin' awa'
To the land o' the leal.

Our bonnie bairn's there, John,
She was both gude and fair, John;
And O! we grudged her sair
To the land o' the leal.

We resented letting her go to the 'land o' the leal', the land where the faithful go: heaven.

O, dry your glistening e'e, John!
My saul langs to be free, John!
And angels beckon me
To the land of the leal.

A JEW WHO GAVE HIS LIFE FOR THE FREEDOM OF THE WORLD

PRIVATE ABRAHAM NATHAN
DEVONSHIRE REGIMENT
DIED 26 OCTOBER 1917 AGED 24
BURIED HOOGE CRATER CEMETERY

The words on the tomb of the Unknown Warrior in Westminster Abbey inspired Mrs Nathan's choice of inscription. The tomb commemorates:

> ... the many
> Multitudes who during the Great
> War of 1914-1918 gave the most that
> Man can give life itself
> For God
> For King and Country
> For loved ones home and Empire
> For the sacred cause of justice and
> The freedom of the world.

Private Nathan was a Londoner. He came from Shoreditch where there was a large Jewish community, and much accompanying anti-Semitism. He was killed on 26 October 1917, a disastrous day according to the regimental history:

> October 26th, 1917, stands out as the worst day the 8th and 9th Devons ever experienced. They had known heavy losses before, at Loos, at Mametz, at Ginchy, but they had never gone into an attack with the scales weighted so heavily against them. ... It was the mud that was Gheluvelt's most effective defence, and the failure of the 8th and 9th to take Gheluvelt was recognised by those in authority as due to no fault of theirs, rather their determination and gallantry were lavishly praised ... the spirit which had led these two battalions to advance so unflinchingly to an attack they could not but realise to be a forlorn hope, represents a triumph of discipline and of esprit de corps. The saddest day in their history, it was, nevertheless, the high-water mark of their endeavour.
>
> *Devonshire Regiment 1914-1918* CT Atkinson

SECOND LIEUTENANT HUGH GORDON LANGTON
LONDON REGIMENT (ROYAL FUSILIERS)
DIED 26 OCTOBER 1917 AGED 32
BURIED POELCAPELLE BRITISH CEMETERY

The War Graves Commission's instructions were clear, if you would like to choose a personal inscription for your relation's headstone it should be limited to 66 characters and, 'It is regretted that special alphabets, such as Greek, cannot be accepted'. This being the case, how did Langton's widow, Mrs Una Mary Langton, get this musical phrase, six notes in the treble clef, accepted as her husband's inscription? The answer is that no one knows but that as in many other cases, the Commission must have used its discretion. Why Langton's 'inscription' consists of a musical notation is easier to answer. He was a musician, a violinist of great promise who was taught by some of the finest teachers in Europe: Otakar Sevcik of Prague and Vienna, Leopold Auer of St Petersburg, and Emanuel Wirth of Berlin, the latter a member of the famous Joachim Quartet. The question of what the notes represent is a much more difficult to answer. They are not part of a tune that anyone has been able to discern and several have tried; in particular they are not from the song *After the Ball* as some have suggested. Langton served with the 4th London Battalion Royal Fusiliers, which suffered terribly in an attack at Poelcapelle on 26 October. He is 'believed to be buried' in Poelcapelle Cemetery where 6,230 of the 7,479 burials are unidentified. According to his medal rolls index card he had been at the front for just sixteen days. Hugh Langton was the only child of John Gordon Langton and Emily his wife. Emily's father, Hugh's grandfather, was German. Langton married Una Mary Broxholme in December 1913 but the couple had no children.

WOULD SOME THOUGHTFUL HAND IN THIS DISTANT LAND PLEASE SCATTER SOME FLOWERS FOR ME

PRIVATE EDWIN GRANT
CANADIAN INFANTRY
DIED BETWEEN 26TH AND 28TH OCTOBER 1917 AGED 33
BURIED TYNE COT CEMETERY

Mrs Grant's plea does not go unheeded. People often drop a flower on her husband's grave, and this is quite apart from the flowers that permanently fill the beds in front of every grave. Far away in Vancouver, British Columbia, one doubts that Bella Grant would ever have been able to do this herself – few made this journey from Canada. Her husband, Edwin Grant, had been born in Aberdeen. He worked there as an engineers' labourer before emigrating to Canada where he became a steel worker. He enlisted in February 1916 and served with the 47th Battalion Canadian Infantry. He was killed sometime between the 26th and the 28th October 1917, the War Graves Commission does not have a firm date. During that period the battalion was in 'close support' at Abraham Heights and took part in the attack there on the 27th.

> 26 October: B Coy moved forward to the NE side of Passchendaele Rd. Lt Hinckesman, 2nd in command of B Coy was killed by a machine gun bullet late in the evening.
> 27 October: During the day the enemy shelled our new line. At night the whole battalion, in conjunction with the 44th was ordered to advance & occupy the ridge in front and throw outposts.
> 28 October: Terrific and intense bombardments of our lines by guns of all calibres marked this day. ... Enemy aeroplanes travelled over our lines throughout the day & directed the enemy's artillery.
>
> Extracts from 44th Battalion War Dairy

After the war, Grant's was one of the thousands of bodies gathered up from the surrounding battlefields and buried in Tyne Cot Cemetery. Of the 11,961 soldiers buried here 8,373 were never unidentified – some of them, no doubt, among the 34,887 missing dead named on the surrounding walls. Seven years after Edwin Grant's death, Bella married his brother, James.

"AND SOME WE LOVED – " OMAR

LIEUTENANT JAMES FRANCIS SIMPSON
MACHINE GUN CORPS
DIED 27 OCTOBER 1917 AGED 19
BURIED LIJSSENTHOEK MILITARY CEMETERY

Despite the fact that the first word of this quotation should be 'For' not 'And' the reference is clear, it comes from Edward Fitzgerald's *Rubaiyat of Omar Khayyam*, which dwells at length on the transient nature of all things, including human life.

> For some we loved, the loveliest and the best
> That from his Vintage rolling Time has prest,
> Have drunk their Cup a Round or two before,
> And one by one crept silently to rest.
>
> Verse XXII

The *Rubaiyat*, with its beautifully expressed, fatalistic philosophy captured the hearts of late Victorian England and readers would easily have recognised this quote, even without the word 'Omar'.

Simpson served with the 20th Company Machine Gun Corps and died of wounds in a Casualty Clearing Station at Lijssenthoek. He was 19. His medal card indicates that he had been at the front for two months.

> Yet Ah, that Spring should vanish with the Rose
> That Youth's sweet-scented Manuscript should close!
>
> Verse XCVI

For God, King and Country

CAPTAIN ROBERT CONINGSBY WILMOT
SHERWOOD FORSTERS NOTTS AND DERBY REGIMENT
DIED 29 OCTOBER 1917 AGED 31
BURIED RUISSEAU FARM CEMETERY

> *The Times*
> 9 November 1917
> Captain Robert Coningsby Wilmot, Sherwood Foresters, killed on October 29, aged 31, was the eldest son of the late Rev. Francis E.W. Wilmot and Mrs Wilmot, of Perrystone Towers, Ross-on-Wye. He had been serving since 1914, and was dangerously wounded in August 1915. Two of his younger brothers have lost their lives in the war, and his two remaining brothers are serving with the Herefordshire Regiment.

Mrs Katharine Wilmot, Robert Wilmot's mother, used the same inscription on the headstones of all three of her sons, Robert, Thomas and Henry – 'For God, King and Country', a centuries-old rallying cry and a common war memorial dedication.

Both Thomas and Henry Wilmot had emigrated to Canada, Thomas in March 1914 to take up farming in Saskatchewan. He returned in October 1914, served with distinction on the Western Front – was awarded a Military Cross for his actions on the 1 July 1916 – was wounded at Thiepval on 24 August and died the next day.

Henry did not return from Canada until December 1915. He enlisted with the Worcestershire Regiment and served in France until April 1917 when he contracted a lung disease from which he died in July 1917.

Robert, a solicitor in Derby, joined the Public Schools Battalion in August 1914 and then took a commission. He served in France from June 1915, was dangerously wounded the next month and didn't return until April 1916. He was killed near Poelcappelle when his dugout received a direct hit.

The Imperial War Museum has two boxes of letters and memorabilia associated with the Wilmot family. There are nearly 300 from Thomas, Henry and Robert and more than a hundred letters of sympathy mixed with newspaper cuttings and much other ephemera.

His brother's keeper

SERGEANT GEORGE HOSTRAWSER
CANADIAN INFANTRY
DIED 31 OCTOBER 1917 AGED 20
BURIED OXFORD ROAD CEMETERY

Sergeant Hostrawser's father, William, chose a brief but effective way of expressing his son's qualities. When God asked Cain where his brother Abel was – just after Cain had killed him – Cain replied, 'I know not: Am I my brother's keeper?' [*Genesis* 4:8] In other words, how should I know and what's more, what do I care? Cain's words have become a shorthand for man's selfishness, his unwillingness to look out for his fellow man. But George Hostrawser was not that sort of man, he *was*, 'His brother's keeper'.

Hostrawser, the youngest of his parents twelve children, enlisted in Brampton, Ontario on 18 December 1915. He served with the 116th Battalion Canadian Infantry. In October 1917 the battalion was in the Weiltje area, near Ypres. It came out of the front line on 28 October but remained in the forward area to provide working parties. This was a dangerous business: four others ranks were killed and two wounded on the 29th, two were killed on the 30th and on 1 November the war diary reported: 'Strength 31 officers, 617 other ranks. Our casualties on the 31st of October were 7 killed and 3 wounded'.

In the twenty-two months he'd been a soldier, Hostrawser, who was 20 and three months when he died, had been promoted to sergeant – reinforcing the sentiment of his father's inscription – he was 'His brother's keeper', a responsible man.

Captain of My Soul

PRIVATE FRANCIS JAMES CAREW
CANADIAN INFANTRY
DIED 31 OCTOBER 1917 AGED 22
BURIED NINE ELMS BRITISH CEMETERY

Private Carew enlisted in September 1915, served with the 85th Nova Scotia Battalion and was wounded on 30 October attacking Passchendaele Ridge. He died the next day. His inscription comes from *Invictus*, a four-verse poem by W.E. Henley, which to many epitomises the British spirit of fortitude in adversity. Private Carew's mother, Lavinia, needed this fortitude. She lived in Halifax, Nova Scotia where on 6 December 1917, five weeks after her son's death, *SS Mont-Blanc* collided with *SS Nimo* in Halifax harbour. *Mont-Blanc*, loaded with high explosives, caught fire and the ensuing blast killed 2,000 people, injured 9,000 more and devastated a large area of the town. Her husband, Francis Joseph Carew, a foreman stevedore, was among the dead. The Carew's lived in Cogswell Street, the location of one of Halifax's four hospitals; it would have been impossible to miss the explosion's burnt, maimed and gashed victims who overwhelmed the town's medical facilities. Did Henley's poem represent Lavinia Carew's own spirit:

Out of the night that covers me,
Black as the pit from pole to pole,
I thank whatever gods may be
For my unconquerable soul.

In the fell clutch of circumstance
I have not winced nor cried aloud.
Under the bludgeonings of chance
My head is bloody, but unbowed.

Beyond this place of wrath and tears
Looms but the Horror of the shade,
And yet the menace of the years
Finds and shall find me unafraid.

It matters not how strait the gate,
How charged with punishments the scroll,
I am the master of my fate,
I am the captain of my soul.

A PRAISE FOR THOSE WHO FOUGHT AND FELL TO SAVE THE EMPIRE'S NAME

PRIVATE JOHN ERNEST ORR
AUSTRALIAN INFANTRY
DIED 1 NOVEMBER 1917 AGED 35
BURIED AEROPLANE CEMETERY

There are some wonderfully vivid descriptions of 'Jack' Orr in his Australian Red Cross Wounded and Missing Enquiry Bureau file:

> Orr was a short, nuggety, red faced man, who had been a butcher before joining the army. Height about 5 ft 7 and a half inches, dark complexion and heavy dark moustache, sturdily built.

Reports about his death vary but these two seem to add up:

> On Nov. 1 when we were on reserves at Passchendaele, Orr was killed by a gas shell which burst right on the Bivy. I did not see him, but Pte. E. Calder B Co. was with Orr when he was killed and can give the details.
>
> G. Taylor, 6650, D Co. 28 Bn A.I.F.
>
> I know that Private J.E. Orr died from the effects of gas on November 1st. 1917, and that he was buried in the field. Whether his grave was ever registered I could not say.
>
> E. Calder, 6556, B Co. 28 Bn A.I.F.

'Buried on the field' means that Orr was buried close to where he died rather than being taken back to a cemetery. His grave was not registered; his body was discovered in an unmarked grave in August 1919 and identified by its disc.

Robert Orr, his elder brother, confirmed his inscription: 'a praise for those who fought and fell to save the Empire's name'. Among those to be included in the praise were not only 'Jack' but another brother, George Wood Orr, killed on 10 October 1916, and Albert Nordstrom aged 21, a brother-in-law killed 31 August 1916, both of them on the Somme.

BEHOLD HOW GOOD AND HOW PLEASANT IT IS FOR BRETHREN TO DWELL TOGETHER IN UNITY (MOTHER)

PRIVATE JAMES ROBERTSON, VC
CANADIAN INFANTRY
DIED 6 NOVEMBER 1917 AGED 35
BURIED TYNE COT CEMETERY

> 27th Battalion Canadian Infantry War Diary
> 6 November 1917: Battalion in front line in front of Passchendaele. Weather dull. Wind N.E. Battalion assembled for the assault and all in position at 4 a.m. Zero hour was 5 a.m. Battalion attacked the village of Passchendaele with the 31st Battalion on the left and the 26th Battalion on the right. All objectives captured at 7.40 a.m. Day spent in consolidating position. 9 machine guns and 76 prisoners were captured. Approximate casualties were: 13 officers and 240 O.R.s.

Private Robertson won a posthumous Victoria Cross in this assault; the citation for his award makes it sound as though he was at a different event.

> When his platoon was held up by uncut wire and a machine gun causing many casualties, Pte Robertson dashed to an opening on the flank, rushed the machine gun and, after a desperate struggle with the crew, killed four and then turned the gun on the remainder, who, overcome by the fierceness of his onslaught, were running towards their own lines ... He inflicted many more casualties among the enemy, and then carrying the captured machine gun ... He selected an excellent position and got the gun into action, firing on the retreating enemy who by this time were quite demoralised by the fire brought to bear on them ... Later, when two of our snipers were badly wounded in front of our trench, he went out and carried one of them in under very severe fire. He was killed just as he returned with the second man.

Robertson's mother chose his inscription. It comes from the first verse of Psalm 133. It was not uncommon for families to use quotations from the bible to veil their criticisms of the war as Mrs Robertson is surely doing here.

I HAVE GIVEN MY LIFE TO PROMOTE PEACE BETWEEN ALL NATIONS

PRIVATE EMANUEL FULTON
CANADIAN INFANTRY
DIED 6 NOVEMBER 1917 AGED 21
BURIED PASSCHENDAELE NEW BRITISH CEMETERY

Private Fulton's mother chose his inscription; it would be interesting to know whether the words were her own or her son's. From the very beginning, many people hoped that this would be the war to end war, which, as H.G. Wells argued, could only be achieved if German militarism was crushed. This is how Emanuel Fulton, or his mother, could believe that he had given his life to promote peace between all nations.

Peace between nations was the aim of the League of Nations, established in 1920 not only to promote peace throughout the world but also to maintain it. The aim was laudable but the execution was flawed and the League was unable to prevent war breaking out in Europe nineteen years later in 1939.

Emanuel Fulton, serving in "C" Company, 31st Battalion Canadian Infantry, part of the Sixth Canadian Infantry Brigade, was killed in the successful capture of the village of Passchendaele on 6 November 1917. The battalion war diary summarised the day:

> Weather - fine and clear.
> At 12 midnight, all were in correct position in assembly area, and communication by lamp established. After a quiet night the attack on the village of Passchendaele was launched at 6.00 am and by 8.00 am the entire town was in the hands of the 6th Canadian Infantry Brigade. The evening found all well established on the eastern outskirts of the town with a well consolidated trench along the whole Brigade front. The loss of Major GD Powis O.C. "C". Coy. early in the day is greatly felt by all ranks.

RANGATIRA PAKU

LIEUTENANT GEOFFREY MAIDENS WALTER GAVIN CATO
ROYAL FLYING CORPS
DIED 6 NOVEMBER 1917 AGED 20
BURIED LIJSSENTHOEK MILITARY CEMETERY

Lieutenant Cato seems to have been very casual about the order in which he gave his Christian names, often rearranging them, but the above order is the way they are given on his birth certificate. He seems to have been quite casual about his names too, on at least one occasion calling himself Reginald Maidens Cato. Born in Napier, Hawkes Bay, New Zealand, Cato embarked for Britain in 1916 to join the Royal Flying Corps. He qualified as a pilot in May 1917 and joined 6 Squadron at Abeele Airfield in June. During the army's attack on Passchendaele Ridge, the Squadron provided vital aerial reconnaissance, which the visibility made very difficult. Detailed to go up on 6 November, Cato took off at 2.55 pm. No one knows whether he completed his patrol or whether it was aborted but within half an hour of take-off his plane broke up and crashed into Lake Dickebusch. Cato and the observer were both killed, drowned. It could have been enemy action or a fault with the machine but there was a suspicion that Cato, known for his fondness for 'stunts', aerobatics, had put the plane into too steep a dive and it had broken up.

Cato's inscription, chosen by his father, is Maori for Little Chief. He wouldn't of course have had an inscription had he not served with the Royal Flying Corps because of the New Zealand Government's ban on them. Their objection, that payment was against the Commission's principle of equality, was exactly the reason the Canadian Government decided to pay for all its soldiers' inscriptions. Nevertheless, there are many reasons why a grave doesn't have a personal inscription and cost will only be one of them. It took many years to construct the cemeteries and in that time parents died, widows remarried and changed their name, families moved and the War Graves Commission lost contact.

SA MORT A LAISSE DANS NOS COEURS UNE PLAIE PROFONDE

PRIVATE ALBERT LARIVIERE
CANADIAN INFANTRY
DIED 6 NOVEMBER 1917 AGED 21
BURIED TRACK X CEMETERY

The French translates as, 'His death has left a deep wound in our hearts'. Sometimes relatives composed inscriptions in French because they wanted the local population to be able to understand what they said. Others wrote in French because that was the language they spoke at home. Albert Lariviere's spoke French at home; they came from Sainte Rosa du Lac, a French settlement in Manitoba.

Recruitment figures show that French-speaking Canadians were less likely to volunteer in what they saw as Britain's war than those whose first language was English, despite the fact that parts of France were actually occupied by the Germans. Many French-speaking Canadians had been in the country for more than a century and felt totally Canadian, their connection to France in the distant past. The war in Europe was nothing to them – and nor was the British Empire. Many English speakers however were more recent arrivals. To them the Empire was worth fighting for; the motherland was in danger and that danger threatened them all.

Lariviere enlisted and served in the 16th Canadian Infantry Battalion, known as the Canadian Scottish. The war diary described events on 6 November:

> Wieltje
> In Billets. Working parties of 50 men furnished. No parades. 1st Brigade attacked this morning and carried all objectives. Weather wet. Enemy shelling area occasionally. Casualties: – 3 O.R's killed; 11 wounded; 1 accidentally wounded; 1 missing.

Albert Lariviere is buried in Track X Cemetery with two other members of the 16th Battalion, both also killed on 6 November 1917. Although not mentioned by name, he must have been one of the '3 O.R's killed'.

In loving memory of My dear husband The Kent and England cricketer

SERJEANT COLIN BLYTHE
KING'S OWN YORKSHIRE LIGHT INFANTRY
DIED 8 NOVEMBER 1917 AGED 38
BURIED OXFORD ROAD CEMETERY

> *The Times*
> Friday November 16th 1917
> A FAMOUS SLOW BOWLER
> Colin Blythe, who has been killed in France by a shell, played his first match for Kent in 1890 being then 20 years of age. In the following season he came to the front as a slow bowler and held his place there until the outbreak of the war put a stop to first-class cricket. In the last 40 years we have had five left-hand slow bowlers of the highest class. Blythe was the youngest of the five. ... His best season was 1909 when in first-class matches he took 215 wickets for 14½ runs each. His most notable work, however, was done in 1907, when he was England's mainstay in the Test matches against South Africa ...

As a member of the Kent Fortress Royal Engineers, a volunteer Territorial unit of the British Army, Blythe was already a soldier when the war broke out. However, his medal index card shows that he was not entitled to the 1914/15 Star, therefore he can't have entered a theatre of war until 1916 when he transferred to the 12th Battalion King's Own Yorkshire Light Infantry, a pioneer battalion. The Order of Battle for the Third Ypres Campaign shows the battalion to have been attached to the 5th Army Troops for work on light railways, which were vital for ensuring constant access to and from the front line for ammunition, casualties and reinforcements. This was dangerous work since it always attracted the attention of the German guns, as it did on the night of 8 November when a shell exploded over the working party Blyth was supervising, killing him and three other soldiers.

Serjeant Colin Blythe's headstone in Oxford Road Cemetery

United with His beloved brothers Osborne & Fred Who fell in 1915

PRIVATE HARRY DYE
KING'S OWN YORKSHIRE LIGHT INFANTRY
DIED 8 NOVEMBER 1917 AGED 27
BURIED OXFORD ROAD CEMETERY

Harry Dye was one of the three soldiers killed with Colin Blythe when a shell exploded over their working party (see previous page). The third of his brothers to be killed, it was his brother William who signed for his inscription.

Robert and Ada Dye had five children: William, Harry, Osborne, Frederick and Edith. In 1911 they were all living at home in 12 Artist Terrace, Lower Wortley, Leeds. Come the outbreak of war Frederick, already a territorial soldier, a member of the 7th Battalion West Yorkshire Regiment, volunteered for foreign service. The battalion landed in France on 14 April 1915 and took part in the attack on Aubers Ridge at the beginning of May. Frederick was killed on the 13th in a battle where poor intelligence, poor communications and poor equipment all contributed to the failure. He is buried in Aubers Ridge British Cemetery. William signed for his inscription too:

> A dearly beloved son
> Who bravely did his duty

Osborne Dye served with the Plymouth Battalion, Royal Marine Light Infantry. This embarked from Devonport for the Dardanelles on 6 February 1915, took part in the raid on the Turkish guns at Kum Kale and Sedd-el-Bahr on 4 March, landed at Y Beach on 25 April and spent the next few weeks trying to capture Krithia, the first day's objective. Osborne was killed on 6 June. He is believed to be buried in Redoubt Cemetery. 'Believed to be' because that's what the records said but, when the British returned to the Peninsular at the end of the war, four years after the evacuation, the weather and wild animals had obliterated all traces of many graves.

Mrs Ada Dye signed for Osborne's inscription. It has a distinctly different tone to the ones William signed for:

> A beloved son
> Worthy of a better fate

OXFORD ROAD
CEMETERY

Son of Malcolm & Marion Gifford of Hudson, New York, USA

GUNNER MALCOLM GIFFORD
CANADIAN FIELD ARTILLERY
DIED 8 NOVEMBER 1917 AGED 21
BURIED BRANDHOEK NEW MILITARY CEMETERY NO. 3

There's a very strange story behind this most normal of inscriptions. Just look at this report from the front page of a New York newspaper on 18 April 1914:

> RICH BOY HELD AS MURDERER
> Malcolm Gifford Jr. seventeen-year-old son of a wealthy manufacturer of Hudson is under arrest here charged with being the 'slayer of mystery' in the tragic murder of Frank J. Chute, chauffeur, April 1, a year ago.

The circumstantial evidence was extremely damning but, even though Gifford was tried twice, neither jury could agree on a verdict. There was, however, a lingering suspicion that the fact that Gifford's parents were extremely wealthy might have had something to do with the outcome.

After the second trial in 1915, Gifford went to College and it was from here that he enlisted in February 1917, just two months before the United States entered the war. After training, Gifford arrived at the front in late September 1917. Barely two months later he was killed by a shell. The *New York Times* reported his death on its front page with the headline:

> MALCOLM GIFFORD KILLED
> Youth twice tried on murder charge dies in France.

Perhaps Gifford would never have escaped his past. But at least his parents didn't attempt to dissociate themselves from him, in fact far from it: they have put both their names and their address on his headstone.

He wore the white flower of a blameless youth

PRIVATE EDGAR BRIERLEY
CANADIAN INFANTRY
DIED 10 NOVEMBER 1917 AGED 35
PASSCHENDAELE NEW BRITISH CEMETERY

The shadow of his loss drew like an eclipse,
Darkening the world. We have lost him: he is gone:
We know him now: ...
... and we see him as he moved,
How modest, kindly, all-accomplished, wise,
... through all this tract of years
Wearing the white flower of a blameless life,

The above, much abbreviated, is an extract from the dedication at the beginning of Tennyson's Arthurian poem, *Idylls of the King*, which, as he wrote, 'I consecrate with tears' to Queen Victoria's consort, Prince Albert.

Brierley, born and brought up in Lancashire, emigrated to Canada before 1911. He served with the 7th Battalion Canadian Infantry and died on 10 November 1917 when the Battalion attacked towards Musselmarkt in the final stage of the Third Ypres campaign. The Battalion war diary provides an interesting insight into the aftermath of a battle:

> It was impossible during the 10th to clear the wounded from the Regimental Aid Post, owing to exceptionally heavy shell-fire, with the result that the Post was crowded with stretcher cases during the night. These were cleared during the 11th by a brigade party of 300 Other Ranks which came up in the early morning, and by 8 p.m. (11th) all wounded of the Brigade had been cleared from Musselmarkt.
>
> Owing to the exhaustion of the men and the constant shell-fire, it was impossible to bury many of the dead and no means were at hand for marking the graves of those that were buried.

Brierley's body was recovered from an unmarked grave in May 1920.

VIEGLAS SMILTIS SVESUMA DUSSI SALDI

PRIVATE OSCAR MARTIN ABRAMSON
CANADIAN INFANTRY
DIED 10 NOVEMBER 1917 AGED 30
BURIED PASSCHENDAELE NEW BRITISH CEMETERY

This inscription is in Latvian and means 'may the earth of a foreign land lie light upon you'. It's a relatively formulaic dedication Latvians use for graves and memorials, the Latvian equivalent of 'May he rest in peace'. The phrase bears a striking resemblance to the Latin formula the Romans put on their graves and memorials, Sit tibi terra levis – may the earth rest lightly on you. It's a sentiment that can be found in English culture too: 'Lie lightly upon my ashes gentle earth', (*Tragedy of Bonduca*, John Fletcher 1579-1625), or as in the quotation from *Annette,* by the Australian poet Robert Richardson (1850-1901):

> Warm summer sun shine kindly here;
> Warm southern wind blow softly here
> Green sod above lie light, lie light –

Oscar Abramson was born in Riga, at that time one of the most advanced and economically prosperous cities in the Russian Empire. He emigrated to Canada where he worked as a tailor in Kingston, Ontario. He enlisted in the 20th Battalion Canadian Infantry, the Central Ontario Battalion, in January 1916, naming his father, Adam Abramson in Riga, as his next-of-kin.

Then thought I To understand this But it was too hard for me

PRIVATE THOMAS LITTLE
SOUTH WALES BORDERERS
DIED 10 NOVEMBER 1917 AGED 21
BURIED PASSCHENDAELE NEW BRITISH CEMETERY

This quote from Psalm 73:15 in the Book of Common Prayer sounds like an inoffensive comment but is probably a criticism of the war if not of the world. Thomas Little's father, Thomas Royal Little, who chose the inscription, was a Consultant Engineer and Naval Architect. An intelligent, wealthy man he was not the sort of person to say that something was too hard for him to understand, unless he meant that the sort of behaviour war encouraged in supposedly civilised people was incomprehensible to him – which is what I would suggest he did mean.

Not much is known about Thomas Little other than that he served with the 1st Battalion South Wales Borderers and went missing on the night of 10 November 1917. Having successfully taken Passchendaele village on the 6th, the Army was desperate to capture the high ground behind it. The 10th was fixed as the date for the attack and the Borderers were detailed to be part of it. The regimental history describes conditions:

> The night was pitch dark, with rain at intervals, the country was a mixture of glue and water, churned up indescribably by the bombardments so that off the duck-board tracks a footing was hard to obtain. In places the duck-boards themselves were under water, and if a man slipped off he usually fell into a deep shell hole full of water and would be lucky to escape alive.

Zero hour was at 5 am. At 7.15 am the first counter-attack began. The regiment held out all morning, harassed by German aeroplanes, but didn't achieve its objectives. By the time the Borderers were relived that evening it had suffered almost 400 casualties killed, wounded and missing. Little was one of the missing, his body not discovered until 23 March 1920 when it was identified by his disc.

OUR BOY
DUTY NOBLY DONE

CORPORAL EDWARD ERNEST STAINSBY
AUSTRALIAN INFANTRY
DIED 10 NOVEMBER 1917 AGED 23
BURIED PASSCHENDAELE NEW BRITISH CEMETERY

King George V sent the following message to the Army on the eve of its departure for France:

> You are leaving home to fight for the safety and honour of my Empire. Belgium, whose country we are pledged to defend, has been attacked and France is about to be invaded by the same powerful foe.
> I have implicit confidence in you my soldiers. Duty is your watchword, and I know your duty will be nobly done.
> I shall follow your every movement with deepest interest and mark with eager satisfaction your daily progress, indeed your welfare will never be absent from my thoughts.
> I pray God to bless you and guard you and bring you back victorious.

This is the origin of the popular inscription, 'Duty nobly done'; it's as if the dead soldier is reporting back to his King.

Edward Stainsby, his brother and his father all served in the war. Father and brother returned but Edward was killed. A witness to the Australian Red Cross Wounded and Missing Enquiry Bureau related what happened:

> We were in the support at Broodseinde Ridge on November 10th and during a gas-shell bombardment two men, of whom Stainsby was one, took cover in the same dug-out. No one knew they were killed until the next morning, and then as they were missing, the dug-out was excavated, and their remains were found, and identified by Captain Ellwood ... by their paybooks. Two temporary crosses were put up. I knew Stainsby very well. He was tall, fair, clean shaven. He came from Richmond.

THROUGH HIS DEATH MANY HAVE LOST MUCH

PRIVATE JOHN JAMES HARGREAVES
MANCHESTER REGIMENT
DIED 10 NOVEMBER 1917 AGED 36
BURIED CEMENT HOUSE CEMETERY

This statement is true of all those bereaved by the war whether the dead man was a potential captain of industry or a general labourer. John Hargeaves was a cotton weaver from Bacup in Lancashire. A married man, he served with the 12th Battalion the Manchester Regiment and was killed in action on 10 November 1917 during the Second Battle of Passchendaele.

Among the many who 'lost much' were the children of Bacup. Ten years after the end of the war, the Bacup war memorial was unveiled in the pouring rain, the local paper remarking that:

> The most touching part of the whole ceremony was said to be the presence of children of men killed in the war and wearing their father's medals. Shivering in the rain and trying to keep back the tears which silently flowed, and grasping lovingly the posies 'In loving memory of Daddy'.

The newspaper listed the names of the children standing shivering in the pouring rain, among them was that of Cyril Hargreaves - Private Hargreaves' son perhaps?

THE MENIN GATE

TO THE ARMIES OF THE
BRITISH EMPIRE WHO STOOD
HERE FROM 1914 TO 1918 AND
TO THOSE OF THEIR NUMBER
WHO HAVE NO KNOWN GRAVE

EPITAPHS FEATURED IN THIS BOOK BY CWGC CEMETERY

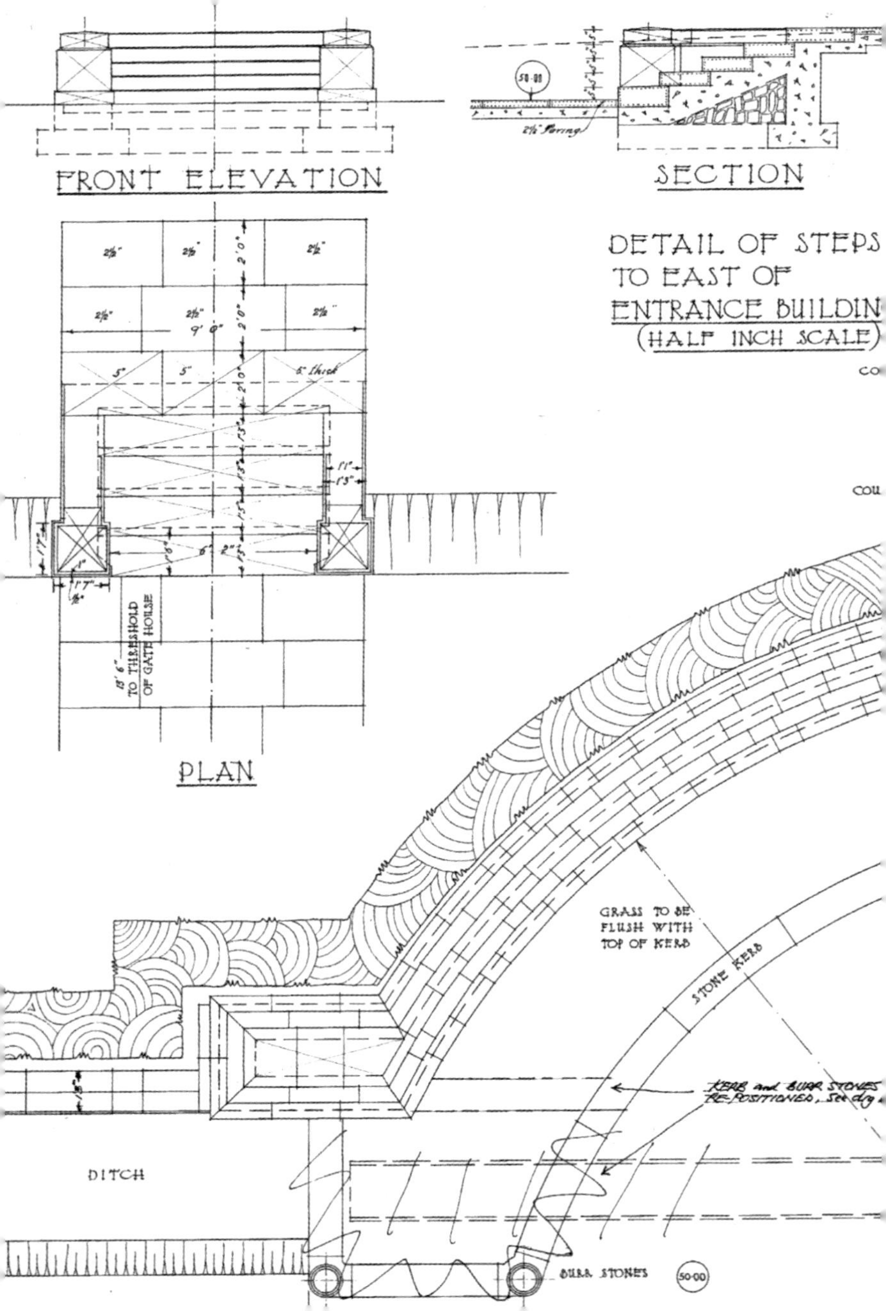

FRONT ELEVATION
SECTION
50-00
2½" Paving
DETAIL OF STEPS
TO EAST OF
ENTRANCE BUILDIN
(HALF INCH SCALE)
2½"
2'0"
9' 0"
5"
5" thick
1'1"
1'3"
1'7"
6' 2"
13' 6"
TO THRESHOLD
OF GATE HOUSE
PLAN
GRASS TO BE
FLUSH WITH
TOP OF KERB
STONE KERB
KERB and BURR STONES
RE-POSITIONED, See dg
DITCH
BURR STONES
50-00